food for every body

Jane Barnes and
Sydney Pemberton

CANCELLED

food for every body
cooking for diabetes the low-GI way

Photography by Brett Stevens

Lothian
BOOKS

Thomas C. Lothian Pty Ltd
132 Albert Road, South Melbourne, 3205
www.lothian.com.au

National Library of Australia
Cataloguing-in-Publication data:

Barnes, Jane A.
    Food for every body : cooking for diabetes the low-GI way.

    ISBN 0 7344 0631 2.

    1. Diabetes - Diet therapy - Recipes. I. Pemberton, Sydney.
    II. Title.

641.56314

Cover design by ektavo
Typeset in 9.5/12.5 pt The Serif 3-Light by ektavo
Printed in China by Imago Productions

Authors' notes

✎ = the *Food for Every Body* symbol = the Glycaemic Load of each recipe.
Some recipes in this book contain significant amounts of carbohydrate,
although they only have a low GI and a Glycaemic Load of 2. To gauge
how your body handles these recipes (or any others), it is strongly
recommended that you do a blood glucose test two hours after eating
the dish. Eating then testing is the best way to help work out what
quantity of carbohydrates you can handle.

Fructose is sweeter than sugar. Fruisana is a readily available brand of
fructose and is recommended as a sugar alternative in this book. When
replacing sugar with Fruisana in your own recipes, you may find that
less Fruisana is required. This means that the overall kilojoule level, as
well as the GI and Glycaemic Load, will be less. In our recipes, we have
already reduced the amount of sugar to a minimum so, by following the
Fruisana version of the recipe, you should enjoy a 'bigger' taste.

For more information on Diabetes go to www.diabetes-australia.com.au

Disclaimer

While the authors have made every effort to ensure that the
information and advice in this book is complete and accurate, neither
the authors nor the publisher shall be liable or responsible for any loss,
injury or damage allegedly arising from any advice contained herein.
The book is not intended as a substitute for consulting your health
practitioner and obtaining medical advice regarding any action that
may affect your well-being.

contents

dedication and acknowledgements

This book is dedicated to all those diabetics we have known who have been our inspiration, we hope we can now inspire you to enjoy a wider variety of delicious and interesting foods.

This book would not have been possible without the generosity of Roche Diagnostics Australia Pty Ltd and Danisco Australia Pty Ltd, makers of Fruisana Fruit Sugar. Thank you also to Mike Williams of Serve for his patience, while developing our *Food for Every Body* symbol counts.

We wish to thank Brett, Marie-Hélène and Wendy for their special input and creativity and of course Averill Chase for her enthusiasm and friendship throughout this project. Finally, a big 'thank you' to our great network of supporters – the family and friends who have always been happy to listen, and help with the tastings as recipes for the book have evolved.

preface

Good food is to enjoy, and the preparation and sharing of meals with friends and family can be one of life's more pleasurable experiences. Eating is something we should all look forward to, diabetics included. Managing diabetes need not spell a social and culinary death sentence.

As recently as 10 years ago, a diagnosis of diabetes was quickly followed by instructions to forgo lots of favourite dishes and stick to plain boring food. Thankfully, today's advice is radically different. New food information, together with better knowledge of how the body regulates blood glucose levels (BGLs), makes a social and gourmet life possible, while doing the 'right thing' by your diabetes.

Our challenge has been to put together delicious ideas that are easy to cook, yet fit in with the latest research for controlling BGLs.

Anyone can happily join your table because eating for blood glucose control is the same as eating for health. That is why this book is called *Food for Every Body*.

Here is a collection of recipes and food ideas to fit most lifestyles and home kitchens. In *Food for Every Body*, we have arranged the recipes by major food groups – potatoes, rice, pasta, grains, and legumes – since regular daily serves of carbohydrates are essential for glucose production and good health. Of course, we have also included some tempting desserts that every body will enjoy.

Our aim is that by the time you have experienced a number of delicious *Food for Every Body* recipes and taken note of our handy tips, you should have sufficient knowledge to be able to adapt and incorporate all of your favourite dishes for everyday eating, even if you have diabetes.

We wish you great tastes, happy eating and good health.

Jane Barnes and Sydney Pemberton

starting off – rating your eating habits

The prospect of change can be daunting, especially if you think that everything you were doing now has to be modified. But don't despair. You probably already have some of the *Food For Every Body* eating habits we recommend; so score yourself on the following quiz. Each question illustrates a desirable eating habit, take note of the ones where you score highly and use these as foundations to build more winning eating goals. It could be reassuring to redo the quiz after using *Food for Every Body* for a while to see how much you have increased your score.

1 Fruits per day? Count as one serve fresh or canned fruit to the same volume as one orange, e.g. an average-sized apple, ½ cup of grapes or a small glass of fruit juice.

Less than 1 serve	score 2	
1-2 serves	score 4	
More than 2 serves	score 6	Score _____

2 Dairy per day? Count as one serve 250 ml milk (or calcium-fortified equivalent), 30 g cheese, a 200 ml tub yoghurt, or 2 scoops dairy ice cream.

Less than 1 serve	score 2	
1-3 serves	score 4	
More than 3 serves	score 6	Score _____

3 Pulses/legumes (baked beans, beans, lentils, chickpeas, etc.) per week? Count as one serve any dish with more than ⅓ cup (canned or re-hydrated).

1 or less serves	score 2	
2 serves	score 4	
More than 2 serves	Score 6	Score _____

4 Nuts per day? Count each ½ tablespoon as a serve.

Negligable or more than 2 serves	score 2	
Less than 1 serve	score 4	
1-2 serves	score 6	Score _____

5 Number of low-GI foods per day? (See page 155 for list of GI foods)

Less than 2 low-GI foods	score 2	
2-4 low-GI foods	score 4	
More than 4 low-GI foods	score 6	Score _____

6 Cups of salad and/or vegetables per day (raw volume), excluding potatoes?

Less than 1 cup	score 2	
1-2 cups	score 4	
More than 2 cups	score 6	Score _____

7 Water per day? Count each 250 ml glass as one serve.

Less than 2 serves	score 2
2-6 serves	score 4
More than 6 serves	score 6 Score _____

8 Regular eating makes appetite control easier.
Score 1 for each time you have a meal or snack per day.

Less than 3 times	score 2
3-4 times	score 4
5 or more times	score 6 Score _____

9 Fish per week? Count as one serve every 50 g fresh or canned fish in any dish.

1 or less serves	score 2
2 serves	score 4
More than 2 serves	score 6 Score _____

10 Your current body weight is an indication of whether you are eating appropriate quantities of food.
Are you:

more than 25% above
or below your
recommended weight?   score 2

5-20 kg above
or below your
recommended weight?   score 4

within 5kg of your
recommended weight?   score 6   Score _____

Total score _____

How did you score?

Less than 24	You are regularly making some winning choices but now is a good time to re-assess your everyday eating patterns.
24-44	A good number of your habits are winning ones, but your BGL and general wellbeing could improve if you developed a few of the high-scoring habits we suggest.
45 or more	Going well! Use *Food for Every Body* for new tastes and combinations.

The scientific reasoning behind our eating targets – and practical solutions for achieving them – is explained throughout the book.

diabetes tech talk

Here are some key facts about blood glucose:
- the average human body contains at least 8 litres of blood, in which there is only about 1½ teaspoons of glucose at any one time
- the hormone insulin is produced in the pancreas and acts like a key, opening up the cell 'doors' so that glucose can go inside, causing blood glucose levels (BGLs) to return to the constant
- after eating a carbohydrate-containing food, we all experience a rise in our BGLs, which should return to normal within two hours
- usually, the body senses extra glucose and signals the pancreas to produce appropriate amounts of the hormone insulin ('the key' which opens the cells). The glucose can then move into the cells, where it can be used for energy.
- our BGLs stay constant, despite being the major fuel for all cells, as there is ongoing topping up (balancing) of the glucose from cell-stored glucose back into the blood, if necessary
- if insulin action is faulty, for whatever reason, then the body does not regulate the BGL correctly – we call this diabetes.

Several things can go wrong with the insulin regulation system:
- the pancreas stops producing insulin altogether (Type I Diabetes)
- the cell 'doorlocks' may not be sufficiently responsive to insulin, that is they become 'insulin resistant', or else the pancreas no longer produces enough insulin to be effective (Type II, Impaired Glucose Tolerance and Gestational Diabetes).

Control of blood glucose, whatever the cause of the diabetes, is achieved by maximising the effectiveness of insulin. As tummy fat is one of the biggest blocks to insulin effectiveness on a day-to-day basis, we can increase the sensitivity of our cells to insulin – whether our own or injected insulin – by:
- moderating fats in our diet and thus reducing tummy fat
- moderating glucose input (load)
- maintaining a consistent intake, making day-to-day control easier.

This is where *Food For Every Body* can be of help.

Diabetes never goes away. With good management, the majority of the time, your BGL can appear normal. Although there is a little more 'balancing' to do if you need to use insulin, the overall principles of day-to-day self-care are the basis for any lifestyle that is geared towards maximising body potential.

The recipes in *Food For Every Body* give you an invaluable tool for the management of blood glucose input and overall good health.

feasting – taking control of your health

Introduction

New fad eating rules, magic food ideas, and extreme regimens promising health, weight loss or diabetic management seem to crop up all the time.

The philosophy of *Food For Every Body* is this: Forget the fads; forget the magic foods. Establish a few appropriate, regular eating habits for long-term health effectiveness.

There should be no need for special foods for diabetes. The well-advertised, basic principles of healthy eating and living for all are the cornerstones for long-term blood glucose management. If there is a magic key, it is how much we eat.

Whether you no longer produce insulin, or what you produce is not functioning properly, foods are still digested in the same way, so our eating principles apply to everyone. By committing time now to developing a few simple healthy habits of food choice and quantity, in the future your blood glucose level (BGL) will automatically be better controlled.

A diabetic diagnosis never goes away. Your aim should be to control your intake so that your blood test results are as near as possible to those of a non-diabetic person.

Whatever your eating goal, food should always be pleasurable. The precise quantity of food you need depends on your activity levels, body size, metabolism, and on whether you are trying to maintain body size or trying to lose body fat. Use the recipes in *Food For Every Body* to find new, enjoyable food solutions that can become regular eating habits, paving the way to lifelong good diabetic health.

The Big Problem – our feast

In terms of quantity, most Australians are eating in feast proportions. Sadly, the human body is not geared for this continual excess, and obesity rates are climbing.

In the past, life was a seesaw between feast and famine. To survive famine, our bodies developed a specific gene, which enabled efficient storing of excess intake as tummy fat. Unfortunately, we have no signal that says 'enough stored'. Nothing tells us to stop eating.

Survival tummy fat is different from other fat stores because it is more 'mobile', ready for the instant 'flight' or 'fight' responses. Picture a continual movement of fat particles in and out of the tummy, travelling through the bloodstream. The more tummy fat you have, the greater the movement. These fat particles interfere with a whole range of normal body functions, particularly insulin activity, as well as stimulating cholesterol/triglyceride production and raising blood pressure.

By reducing tummy fat, you will make it easier for insulin and other factors to work and so improve your BGL.

The good news is you do not have to become a 'skinny mini' to see improved insulin action. You will achieve improved results even with a 10 per cent reduction in body weight or, in practical terms, if you drop one dress size or two notches on your belt. You can manage that!

Identifying the right quantity of today's feast

The big question is how much food do we need? There is no simple answer. With most foods, some is vital for health yet too much or too little does us no good. Understanding our body's basic needs is the start to working out the quantities we should consume.

The general feast

Some points to remember:

- almost all foods and beverages contain useable food fuel (kilojoules). There is no magic food known that will take away kilojoules. However drinking water is almost magic, since it helps fill the stomach, thereby reducing space and appetite
- hunger pangs are often a poor indication of how much to eat, particularly if previous large meals have stretched the stomach
- long gaps between food intake mean we become over-hungry, then we overeat. Small frequent eating controls hunger and shrinks the stomach
- all foods not used for basic metabolism and/or extra activity will be converted and stored as excess fat
- by eating 10 per cent less food than you are now eating, you will shed tummy fat. Try cutting crusts off sandwiches, or leaving 10 per cent of that dessert.

The carbohydrate feast

Glucose is the only type of fuel our brain cells can use, as well as being the preferred food fuel for all other cells. Foods which, on digestion, produce glucose, are classed as carbohydrates and are the only foods which can add to blood glucose supply.

Insulin is the chemical 'key' which opens the 'doors' on body cells so glucose can pass from the blood into the cells to be used as fuel. Fats in food, or stored in the tummy, block the 'lock and key' action of insulin, interfering with the processing of glucose.

Originally, the standard advice to diabetics was to avoid all carbohydrates. The rationale was that if there was no glucose entering the system, then there would be no need for insulin to manage BGLs. Such a diet could not work long-term because of the central role of glucose in cell functioning. That is why today's fad for longer-term low-carbohydrate diets is not ideal.

The focus then moved to 'counting' carbohydrate intake. It was assumed that a certain amount (number of grams) of carbohydrate in one food would have the same blood glucose effect as an equal amount of carbohydrate in any other food. In practical terms, if lunch today was a ham and salad sandwich with two slices of wholegrain bread, containing about 30 g of carbohydrate, then tomorrow you should obtain a similar blood glucose effect if you eat any combinations containing about the same amount of carbohydrate; e.g. fresh tomato soup with a wholegrain dinner roll; chicken salad with a small cup of rice salad; a noodle dish with 1 cup of noodles; or a tub of diet yoghurt and a cup of strawberries.

About 20 years ago, with the introduction of the first personal blood glucose monitoring equipment, scientists caught up with what most diabetics already knew – these equivalents did not work in real life. Today, BGL monitoring is the recommended method of checking appropriate intake.

Carbohydrate tech talk

Here are some key facts about glucose:

- carbohydrates are glucose-producing foods

- glucose is vital for good health – it is the essential fuel for all cells

- even if our glucose-handling system is impaired, it is crucial that we find a way to take in glucose

- the glycaemic index (GI) rating of a glucose food indicates the rate that its glucose is released into the blood (digested)

- although low GI foods are easier for the body to handle, they cannot be consumed in unlimited quantities. This is because all carbohydrates produce glucose and any excess will be converted into fat.

- the impact of different foods on blood glucose is measured by multiplying the quantity of carbohydrate content by the GI and dividing the result by 100. This concept is called the Glycaemic Load.

- if the same quantity of carbohydrate exists in two different foods but the GI varies, creating a different Glycaemic Load for each food, to achieve a similar Glycaemic Load you would need to consume either:
  1 serve of a low GI food OR
  2/3 serve of a medium GI food OR
  1/2 serve of a high GI food.

- while calculating the Glycaemic Load for a single carbohydrate food is relatively straightforward, it is more complex for a dish containing several different carbohydrate foods.

To assess the blood glucose impact of each recipe in *Food for Every Body*, an equivalence measure was developed, comparing the relative Glycaemic Load of each dish against the likely blood glucose impact of eating a wholegrain sandwich.

How to use the *Food for Every Body* symbol

We have created a special at-a-glance symbol ⌀ for you, representing the Glycaemic Load of each recipe in *Food for Every Body*. This can be interpreted thus:

⌀ = a Glycaemic Load of 1

⌀⌀ = a Glycaemic Load of 1½

⌀⌀ = a Glycaemic Load of 2

Using the *Food for Every Body* symbol in conjunction with home BGL monitoring will help you develop an understanding of how different recipes containing carbohydrates affect your system.

Here are some examples of how the *Food for Every Body* symbol can guide your choices:

- Madras Pork Wrap with Yoghurt and Mint (see page 127) is low GI and contains 29 grams of carbohydrate. Its Glycaemic Load is 1.
- Creole Beef, Corn and Borlotti Bean Bake (see page 129) is also low GI and contains 38 grams of carbohydrate. Its Glycaemic Load is also 1.

As a result you could select either of these dishes for the same blood glucose effect, even though one contains more carbohydrate that the other.

- By comparison, Lamb Korma with Mango Chutney on Turkish Bread (see page 110) is medium GI and contains 22 grams of carbohydrate. Its Glycaemic Load is 1½. Selecting this dish instead of the Madras Pork or Creole Beef would have a different blood glucose effect.

The effect on the Glycaemic Load of substituting a much lower GI ingredient can be seen in the dessert section where Fruisana fruit sugar (low GI) has been suggested in place of regular sugar (a high medium-GI).

- The Hazelnut and Lemon Cake (see page 151) has a Glycaemic Load of ½ if you use sugar, whereas, using Fruisana, it has a Glycaemic Load of ¼ for the same size serving. Using Fruisana, the recipe has a lower blood glucose impact.

The value of monitoring BGLs

Select a recipe. You will notice that we have included a full nutrient count as well as the ⌀ symbol after each one. For a comparison of the BGL impact, you should look at the symbol, remembering that one ⌀ means a recipe will have a similar BGL impact to 2 slices of wholegrain bread. Enjoy eating the dish and then check your BGL two hours later.

Remember everyone is different. Only by monitoring your own BGL can you effectively begin to enjoy all food, gradually learning the exact effect of certain foods and portion sizes on your system.

There is no single right amount of carbohydrate. The amount you need depends on many personal factors, not the least of which is how active you are about to be. If you are planning a day's heavy gardening, a big night out dancing or an exhausting game of netball or football, you will need more available glucose than if your afternoon or evening is to be spent watching the television or sitting in front of a computer.

Of course, there is inevitably a degree of 'guesstimation' in assessing the impact of food on your BGL because of innumerable other food factors influencing the GI. BGL monitoring reduces the guesswork, making it easier to keep your BGL under control. Good luck - enjoy experimenting with our recipes.

The Fat Feast

Fat has become this century's 'dirty' word. Moreover, if a food contains no fat or is low in fat, the assumption is you can eat as much of it as you like – forgetting that excess carbohydrates and proteins will also add tummy fat. Interestingly, stored fat can only be effectively used up when adequate carbohydrate is circulating, a good reason for eating regular, small amounts of carbohydrate foods.

Another often-forgotten fat fact is that some fats are vital for life, as the human body cannot self-manufacture particular fats. If deprived of these vital fats, the body reacts as if it is in famine and changes its metabolism to 'save' fat stores. Given that fat restrictions are often aimed at trying to use up fat stores, inadvertently causing the body to save them seems counterproductive!

Although olive oil contains some of these vital fats and other more 'body-friendly' fats, and so is regarded as 'good for you', the recent trend to douse everything in it – likewise canola oil – is not entirely beneficial. Olive oil contains the same kilojoules per gram as suet, namely 37. Take a balanced approach. Olive oil is a good choice, but avoid excessive use.

Recent research indicates that, for diabetics, insulin appears to be sensitive to large amounts of fat released from a meal as well as to excess tummy fat. Diabetics are particularly sensitive to – and do not cope well with –

saturated fats (see More about Fats, pages 156-7), so keeping control of intakes of all fats is a winning strategy.

Fat can accentuate many flavours, so reduction in fat levels in cooking will result in different tastes. Experience tells us that if you decide to learn a new habit, you should allow yourself three months to become very used to the new tastes.

So far, we've established that no fat or too little fat is not good and equally, in terms of kilojoules, too much fat is a problem. To achieve the right balance, both for healthy general eating and for managing diabetes, follow these guidelines:

- have some fat, but avoid foods dripping with fat – even 'good' fats
- minimise your use of processed foods with high saturated fat levels by reading the labels
- mainly use fats such as canola oil, olive oil, sesame oil or walnut oil
- consume small amounts of nuts daily – averaging one heaped tablespoon
- increase consumption of foods containing protective omega-3 fats (see More about Fats, pages 155-7), such as salmon, tuna, sardines, nuts, enriched eggs and breads, etc.
- keep saturates to 30 per cent of the total fat intake.

Our recipes combine all these guidelines making them ideal for every body.

The importance of protein and other vital nutrients
The protein feast

The protein in foods is used for the daily processes of cell growth – in the young – as well as repair and restoration throughout life. This takes place by a simple recycling process. The building bricks of all proteins are amino acids. These are joined together in various combinations and numbers. When a protein is digested, it is separated out into its individual amino acids. Then each of these are re-built into our own protein units. Unfortunately, although there are some of us who would like the body to do more restoration, eating more protein will not make that happen!

Recently, people have recognised that when they include more than usual amounts of protein in a meal, this can make them feel fuller. Consequently, more diets now emphasise protein. The rationale is clear – feel full and you are less likely to overeat.

This works up to a point but excess protein, like excess carbohydrates and fats, will still be converted to storage fat. Again, there is a fine line between needs/benefits and excess.

The protein serving sizes recommended in *Food For Every Body* will give you an idea of what we believe are the amounts most of us need.

Vitamins, minerals and other 'active nutrients'

There are many biochemical substances that occur naturally in tiny amounts in our foods which are vital for healthy body functioning. These are fascinating and important elements – no doubt plenty more are yet to be discovered – and we have much to learn about how they function and interact.

Despite the doubts often voiced, today's food supply still contains excellent levels of these vital nutrients.

Not all foods contain the same elements. The colour of a vegetable, for instance, is significant, as each colour relates to one of these vital substances, called 'phytochemicals' (protectors). To cover all your phytochemical needs, try to have at least four different colours on you main meal plate. What an attractive health recommendation!

Different foods contain different essential vitamins and minerals so our best advice is to go for variety. It's the surest way to guarantee you pick up all the vitamins, minerals and other active nutrients you need. Variety may be both the spice and saviour of life.

In order to get enough variety you should include the following in your daily diet:
- some wholegrain cereal products
- at least two fruit servings
- 2½ cups of salad and/or vegetables
- lean meat and dairy foods.

Lean meats are great vitamin and mineral stores. The serves in our recipes fit the bill perfectly. Dairy foods are proving to be more and more important as the best calcium source available, as well as being a source of protein, vitamins and other vital nutrients.

In *Food For Every Body*, we have included as wide a range of foods as possible. We know you will enjoy the new tastes and food experiences.

right: lamb pie with spicy potato topping, recipe on page 47

frequently asked questions

Our eating mantra is, 'You can always win'. Your food choices may not always be ideal, but as long as what you end up eating or drinking is better than before, you are winning.

Lots of little wins add up to big gains (or losses, if fat wastage is you goal). You do not have to starve; you do not have to totally deny yourself in order to manage your diabetes. By making small concessions – and always congratulating yourself on each of these – in time you will find that you have established more of the eating habits we have been suggesting. With each FAQ, we suggest a winning strategy.

What do I do when I am hungry?

Firstly, avoid hunger. It's not rocket science – if you are hungry, it's almost impossible to eat well or eat moderately. When there are long gaps between meals or snacks, you become hungry and then overeat, or 'mis-eat'.

That being said, there is a big difference between:
- grazing – which we define as picking up food at any time or any place; and
- planned regular eating – so that mentally and physically you become used to smaller amounts.

Winning strategy
Eat some food about every three hours. Planned frequent eating makes it easier to control what you eat. This also helps with balancing blood glucose levels (BGLs), because, with diabetes, your body cannot handle large loads of glucose-producing foods well.

What if I am really hungry?

Sometimes your body will literally be fighting to make you eat more than you really need. Your body is 'programmed' to respond to an absence of food as if you are in a starvation situation and will prompt you to compensate for that. If you sit down and eat in this state, the chances are you will overeat.

Winning strategy
Eat slowly so your brain has time to register that you are eating, and your stomach has time to register that it is filling up. Drink water with food to add extra 'bulk', and fill up with salads and lots of other low-carbohydrate vegetables.

So what's the right amount to eat?

This is the 64-million-dollar question. Unfortunately there is no single easy answer. The right amount to eat is:
- the quantity of food that provides all the food nutrients your body needs to function properly
- the amount that provides energy quantities so you either use up stored body fat or maintain an appropriate size.

Obviously, the more active you are, the more you can eat without accumulating fat or overloading your system. There is however a minimum 'core' quantity of foods required to meet all basic body functions, so we have tailored the serving sizes in *Food For Every Body* to meet that level.

Winning strategy
Get moving. Every extra pace you take each day uses more kilojoules. Counters, such as pedometers, are a great tool because seeing that you have achieved more steps each day will motivate you to keep moving, so what you eat is more likely to balance with your energy output.

left: raspberry parfait, recipe on page 147

What is a normal meal size?

It is becoming harder to judge what is a normal serving size. Wherever you look, meals are big. In the last 30 years, average commercial serves have been 'upsizing', so larger portions are looking more 'normal'.

Yet, because we sit all day, drive cars, and use labour-saving devices, our energy output is diminishing almost as quickly as our food intake is increasing. What most of us require is less rather than more.

Winning strategy
Learn to leave food or serve yourself less. Although it is hard for many of us at first, leaving 10 per cent of all foods usually eaten is enough to significantly lower total intake.

Is alcohol in or out?

Many of us enjoy alcohol so we need to understand a couple of points:
- alcohol is essentially a poison to the human system which, fortunately, our livers can process and neutralise
- alcohol is, in effect, processed into fat. While this is not strictly accurate, imagine every standard drink you consume has a similar impact on your body as eating 1½ teaspoons of fat.

Safety issues aside, too much alcohol consumption, on a long term basis, cannot help BGLs.

Winning strategy
Alcohol Free Days (AFDs) give the liver time to 'recover' from the hard work of neutralising the alcohol and are better than trying to reduce intakes daily.
- *make at least four days a week AFDs*
- *drink your alcohol for taste not thirst; quench your thirst with water (soda, mineral or tap), or soft drinks*

- *aim to drink at least 2 litres of water or 1 litre of water and another litre of diet soft drinks daily. Becoming used to this amount of non-alcoholic fluid trains you to feel thirsty so you naturally want to drink more*
- *volunteer to be the 'designated' driver when you go out, so you will be forced to keep your intake moderate.*

How about sugar?

It used to be thought that diabetes was caused by eating sugar. Certainly, consuming lots of sugary (high-sucrose) foods places a large glucose load on your body. But the major problem may be that this can add to tummy fat stores, indirectly inhibiting your body's ability to use insulin.

Sugar facts:
- sucrose has a GI of about 64
- sugar is not that filling. A slightly rounded tablespoon (20 grams) is the equivalent of two slices of wholegrain bread on your system
- many sugary foods, such as chocolate, cakes, and so on, also contain fats, which potentially contribute more tummy fats to your body
- fructose is sweeter than sugar, so often less is required to achieve the same sensation of sweetness as sugar. It also has a much lower GI, which can be important in reducing the Glycaemic Load. Fructose sugar replacements such as Fruisana are available nowadays.

Winning strategy
Go for quality not quantity. Buy a small piece of really good chocolate which you can savour rather than a whole bar of cheaper, less enjoyable chocolate. Some sugar helps the taste and texture of foods and, when mixed with other low-GI ingredients, it will not overload your system.

What about the sugar listed on the Nutrition Information Panel (NIP) of processed foods?

Sugar is the technical term for a number of carbohydrates that occur naturally in foods, e.g. lactose in milks, maltose in grains, fructose and glucose in fruits and vegetables. It also refers to the sucrose that manufacturers add to food as sugar. All of these are quantified simply as sugar on the NIP.

So a commercial food that appears to be high in sugar may not necessarily contain added sugar. An example is yoghurt. The carbohydrate lactose is listed as sugar. Interestingly, yoghurt is one of the lowest GI foods around at 14. Some flavoured yoghurts do have added sugar but, even then, their GI only goes up to about 33.

Winning strategy
When you read labels, it is wise not to focus on just one nutrient. The overall kilojoule level of a food is usually a better guide as to whether its ingredients may be excessive. Even then, you still need to take into account how big the serve is.

Antioxidants – what are they and where can I get them?

The terms 'antioxidants' and 'protective nutrients' refer to a range of phenomenally active and powerful chemicals that occur in many foods.

An enormous number of reactions take place in the body every second, many linked to oxygen reactions that produce damaging by-products. Antioxidants neutralise these by-products, thereby protecting the system.

Fruits and vegetables contain many of the known antioxidants, with different colours tending to indicate high concentrations of different antioxidants.

Winning strategy
One main group of antioxidants is found in fruits, vegetables and nuts. Each day make sure you include the following in your diet:
- *at least 2 fruit serves*
- *over 2½ cups of salad and or vegetables (eating a colourful range of vegetables ensures you get most of the vital protectors)*
- *a few nuts (about ½ tablespoon).*

What about sodium?

The common name for sodium is salt. Traditionally, salt is added to food to heighten flavour. Yet sodium occurs naturally in all foods. It is possible, without realising it, to consume quite large amounts of sodium daily from foods that are not necessarily very salty to taste. The human system tries to keep an even level of sodium in the body. A high intake causes the body to battle to rid itself of the excess. That can stress kidneys and cause raised blood pressure, something to which diabetics are highly vulnerable.

Winning strategy
Rather than adding salt to your food, stock up on herbs and spices and try different combinations of these for taste. Food For Every Body introduces an exciting range of no-salt flavours to give taste and satisfaction.

Research shows that up to 75 per cent of our salt intake may come from processed foods, so check the NIP when purchasing them. Wherever possible, select processed foods with low sodium content. Also look out for products labelled 'low-salt' or with the Heart Foundation tick – both indicate that these products meet stringent criteria for sodium content.

menu ideas

We regard planning weekly menus as liberating. Once you have made your choices – and these are likely to be varied and balanced because the planning process encourages you to think of plenty of options – you only have one shopping expedition, which makes good economic sense. And there are other bonuses if you have a plan. For example, it is easy to leave instructions for others to help, should they arrive home first!

kitchen basics

There are a few staple ingredients and foods which we recommend you always keep to hand. Having these ingredients automatically gives you more flexibility to make a nutritious and satisfying meal at the last minute.

Store cupboard ingredients

Cocoa	dark, and good quality (small amount for great taste)
Flour	wholemeal, plain and self-raising
Fish	canned salmon; sardines; tuna
Fruisana	the lower-GI sugar alternative
Fruits	canned in own juice or with no-added-sugar: apricots; peaches; prunes; etc.
Fruit dried	apricots, cranberries (crasins); currants; raisins; sultanas
Herbs/spices	small amounts – keep in dark place as these do go off
Legume/pulses	canned or dried – borlotti beans; butter beans; cannelloni beans; chickpeas; kidney beans; lentils
Milks	long-life skim; canned low-fat condensed and evaporated; lite coconut milk
Noodles	dried but not instant (as they contain high saturated fat)
Nuts	almonds; brazils; pecans; pine nuts; pistachios; walnuts
Oil	olive oil (virgin); canola; sesame
Pasta	dried
Rice	Basmati; fast-cooking rice, such as Sunwhite™ clever rice
Rolled oats	raw
Sauces	reduced-sodium soy sauces; sweet chilli; curry paste; tomato; Worcestershire
Vegetables	canned beetroot; corn; new potatoes; tomatoes, whole and chopped

Refrigerator ingredients

Cheese	feta; quality Parmesan; ricotta
Milk	buttermilk; reduced-fat milk
Eggs	omega-enriched eggs
Yoghurt	plain, reduced-fat

Freezer ingredients

Pastry	filo
Frozen vegetables	peas; corn; beans
Frozen fruits	berries

Fresh basics

Onions	white; red
Garlic	
Green onions	
Salad ingredients	bagged, pre-washed lettuce is a great stand-by
Herbs	
Lemons	

The simplest food needs little accompaniment other than freshly bought seasonal vegetables and fruits. Buy fresh herbs or grow your own – there is nothing more satisfying than adding fresh rosemary to grilled lamb, or basil to simple pasta dishes.

recipes for every body
potatoes

The range of potatoes sold in Australian shops these days has increased well beyond the Desirees, Pontiacs and unwashed. Unfortunately, to date, almost all the potatoes available have GI ratings in the high range. To overcome this we have concentrated on developing recipes that include a balance of potatoes and other ingredients that produce a lower overall Glycaemic Load.

Young, or new, potatoes do have a lower GI than most other potatoes as their starch granules are less mature in structure. If your young potatoes are new, the skin will easily peel off when gently scraped with a round-bladed knife.

Sweet potatoes, although tubers, are not from the same botanical family as regular potatoes. Fortunately for us, however, they have a much lower GI. We have therefore included a number of recipes using sweet potatoes.

Choose potatoes that are firm, well shaped for their variety, and blemish-free.

Main crop potatoes are generally firm. New potatoes have the highest vitamin C content. Soil-covered potatoes will have a longer storage life.

A green tinge indicates that the potato has been exposed to light for too long. Cut this part off or discard the potato.

Storing potatoes

Store potatoes in a cool, dark dry cupboard, on an open storage rack, in a basket or keep in hessian or paper bags. Plastic bags tend to make potatoes sweat, so always remove them from these bags straight after shopping. The moisture of the refrigerator can also make potatoes sweat and go mouldy. Warm conditions, however, can make potatoes sprout.

Varieties of potato and their uses

Bintje – boiling, mashing and gnocchi
Desiree – boiling, mashing, salad, gnocchi
King Edward – mashing, baking
Kipfler – boiling, salad
Nicola – boiling, mashing, salad, soup
Pink fir apple – boiling, salad
Pontiac – boiling, mashing, baking, chips, soup, gnocchi
Red sweet potato – soups, salads, mashing, baking
Roseval – boiling, mashing, soup, gnocchi
Russet – baking, chips
Sebago – boiling, mashing, baking, chips, soup, gnocchi
Spunta – boiling, mashing, baking, chips, soup, gnocchi
Viking – boiling, mashing, baking, gnocchi
White sweet potato – mashing, baking, soups
(has a dry, crumbly texture when cooked).

contents

vegetable, potato and pasta soup with wholegrain croutons

serves 4

1 tablespoon virgin olive oil

2 parsnips, peeled and cut into small chunks

1 leek, washed and thinly sliced

2 sticks celery, thinly sliced

2 cloves garlic, crushed

4 cups chicken stock

4 potatoes, peeled and cut into small chunks

2 tablespoons tomato paste

200 g broad beans (shelled or frozen and defrosted)

100 g dried angel's hair pasta, broken into 10 cm pieces

1 cup wholegrain croutons

2 tablespoons finely chopped black Kalamata olives

2 tomatoes, finely chopped

1 In a saucepan, heat oil and cook parsnip, leek, celery, and garlic over a gentle heat for 6-8 minutes, stirring occasionally.

2 Add stock, potatoes and tomato paste and bring to the boil. Cook at a simmer for 30 minutes until potatoes are just tender.

3 Add broad beans and pasta and cook for 10-15 minutes until pasta is tender.

4 Ladle soup into deep bowls and garnish with wholegrain croutons, olives and tomatoes.

Winning tip
These vegetable winter soups are great pre-or post-exercise, when the body needs carbohydrates.

GLYCAEMIC LOAD 2½

Per serve	
Energy	1670 kJ
Protein	17 g
Fat	7 g
Carbohydrate	59 g
Fibre	11 g
GI	Medium

creamy potato and pumpkin corn chowder

serves 4

2 tablespoons canola oil

2 onions, peeled and finely chopped

500 g pumpkin, peeled and cut into small chunks

500 g potatoes, peeled and cut into small chunks

4 cups chicken stock

1 x 440 g can creamed corn

½ tablespoon worcestershire sauce

½ cup low-fat milk

2 tablespoons finely chopped chives

2 tablespoons crème fraîche or yoghurt

1 Heat oil in a saucepan then cook onion over a gentle heat until soft. Add pumpkin, potatoes and stock and slowly bring to the boil. Simmer for 10-15 minutes until vegetables are just tender.

2 Add creamed corn, worcestershire sauce and milk. Heat through for 5-10 minutes then stir in chives.

3 Ladle into soup bowls and garnish with a little crème fraîche or yoghurt.

GLYCAEMIC LOAD 2¼

Per serve	
Energy	1690 kJ
Protein	15 g
Fat	12 g
Carbohydrate	53 g
Fibre	8 g
GI	Medium

potato pancakes topped with rocket and smoked salmon

serves 4

2 medium-sized potatoes
   (Nicola, Sebago, Pontiac, Bintje, Roseval, King Edward)
1 tablespoon chives, finely chopped
pinch of salt
freshly ground black pepper
1 omega-enriched egg, lightly beaten
2 tablespoons self-raising flour
2 tablespoons light olive oil for frying
1 handful baby rocket leaves
4 slices smoked salmon, cut into thin strips
¼ cup crème fraîche or plain low-fat yoghurt
cracked black pepper
2 green onions, roughly chopped, for garnish

1 Peel potatoes then grate into a mixing bowl. Transfer grated potato to a sieve and place over mixing bowl. Squeeze out as much moisture as possible.
2 In a separate bowl, mix chives, salt, pepper, lightly beaten egg and flour. Stir in drained potatoes and mix well.
3 Heat oil in a non-stick frypan and spoon heaped tablespoons of potato mixture into the pan. Flatten out with a spatula. Cook until lightly browned on bottom side, then flip over to brown the other side, about 3-4 minutes each side. Continue cooking the pancakes until there are about 8.
4 Top each pancake with rocket and smoked salmon and garnish with crème fraîche, cracked black pepper and chopped green onions.

GLYCAEMIC LOAD ¾

Per serve	
Energy	860 kJ
Protein	10 g
Fat	12 g
Carbohydrate	13 g
Fibre	2 g
GI	Medium

fish, leek and potato pie

serves 4

300 g small new potatoes, cut into small chunks
freshly ground black pepper
2 tablespoons chicken, fish or vegetable stock
2 large leeks, washed and sliced into rings
250 g fresh fish fillets (Atlantic salmon, ocean trout,
    deep sea perch or Nile), skin and bones removed
2 tablespoons chopped chives
1 tablespoon finely chopped parsley

Topping
200 g low-fat ricotta cheese
1 tablespoon lite sour cream
1 omega-enriched egg
ground black pepper

1 Preheat oven to 200°C. Parboil potatoes for 10-15 minutes until still firm, then drain and season well with pepper to taste.
2 In a non-stick frypan, cook leeks in stock for 3-4 minutes over a gentle heat until soft. Cut fish into small chunks. Place in a bowl with potatoes, leeks, chives and parsley and mix well.
3 Lightly grease an oven dish. Spoon in fish mixture. Blend topping ingredients and spread over fish mixture.
4 Bake for 25-35 minutes until topping is lightly browned and fish is cooked through. Serve with steamed vegetables or salad on the side.

GLYCAEMIC LOAD ½

Per serve	
Energy	1040 kJ
Protein	22 g
Fat	11 g
Carbohydrate	13 g
Fibre	4 g
GI	Low

thai-style prawn, vegetable and noodle salad

serves 4

1 large sweet potato (600 g), peeled and diced
1 cup diced pumpkin
1 cup broccoli in small florets
2 bundles dried egg noodles
16 green prawns, peeled leaving tails intact, and de-veined
2 tablespoons roughly chopped fresh coriander for garnish
oil spray

Dressing
3 tablespoons lime juice
2 teaspoons fish sauce
3 tablespoons light olive oil
1 teaspoon finely chopped lemongrass
2 small fresh red chillies, de-seeded and finely chopped
1 clove garlic, crushed
1 tablespoon chopped fresh coriander
2 green onions, finely chopped

1 For dressing, combine all ingredients in a bowl and mix well. Put aside.
2 Place a large bamboo steamer over a wok of boiling water. Steam sweet potato for about 7 minutes, then add pumpkin and cook for about 3 minutes. Add broccoli and steam until just tender. Remove all vegetables, refresh under cold water then drain well.
3 Cook noodles in a large saucepan of boiling water for about 5 minutes until just tender. Drain and put aside.
4 Heat a non-stick frypan and spray with a little oil. Stir-fry prawns until just changed in colour (2-3 minutes).
5 In a large bowl, combine sweet potato, pumpkin, broccoli, noodles and prawns. Whisk dressing ingredients and pour over salad. Garnish with sprigs of coriander and serve at room temperature in deep noodle bowls.

GLYCAEMIC LOAD 2

Per serve	
Energy	2020 kJ
Protein	26 g
Fat	15 g
Carbohydrate	56 g
Fibre	5 g
GI	Low

roasted sweet potato and beetroot salad with tuna

serves 4

1 bunch beetroot, trimmed and washed
1 large sweet potato (about 400 g)
1 small red onion, peeled and thinly sliced
1 tablespoon virgin olive oil
4 cups mixed salad leaves
1 x 200 g can tuna in brine, drained and flaked

Dressing
¼ cup orange juice
1½ teaspoons finely grated orange zest
1½ teaspoons honey
1½ teaspoons balsamic vinegar
1 teaspoon Dijon mustard
salt
freshly ground black pepper

1 Preheat oven to 200°C. Cut beetroot into quarters, if really large. Wrap in aluminium foil, place on a baking tray and roast in oven for 30-40 minutes until tender.
2 Remove from oven and cool a little. Slip skins off beetroot and cut into medium chunks.
3 Cut sweet potato into medium chunks and toss with onion and oil. Place in a shallow baking tin and roast in oven for 20 minutes until lightly browned. Remove from oven and cool a little.
4 Whisk together dressing ingredients and put aside. In a salad bowl, combine beetroot, sweet potato, onion, mixed salad leaves and tuna. Pour over dressing and serve.

GLYCAEMIC LOAD ¾

Per serve	
Energy	920 kJ
Protein	15 g
Fat	6 g
Carbohydrate	25 g
Fibre	6 g
GI	Low

sweet potato and zucchini pancakes

serves 4 (makes about 8 pancakes)

1 large (400g) sweet potato
2 medium zucchini, grated
2 omega-enriched eggs
½ cup buttermilk
100 g (¾ cup) wholemeal self-raising flour
spray oil for greasing

1 Peel and cook sweet potato (microwave for 6 minutes or parboil for 8 minutes). Cool then grate.
2 Combine potato with zucchini, eggs, buttermilk and self-raising flour. Mix well and refrigerate for about 30 minutes.
3 Heat a non-stick frypan and spray with oil. Spoon out about ¼ cup mixture, flatten with spatula and cook until browned. Turn and cook other side until golden and cooked through. Place on plate and store in warm oven. Repeat for rest of mixture.
4 Serve topped with food from the grill, such as fish steaks, sausages or rump steak, and serve with green salad on the side.

> **Winning tip**
> *We love buttermilk. Nutritionally, it is a low-GI food that is low in fat yet extremely high in calcium, has a non-acidic taste and works very well as an ingredient. Originally, buttermilk was the liquid left over when milk was churned to make butter. This explains why it is so low in fat yet has all the other goodies from the milk.*

GLYCAEMIC LOAD 1¼

Per serve	
Energy	900 kJ
Protein	20 g
Fat	4 g
Carbohydrate	33 g
Fibre	5 g
GI	Low

seafood, leek and potato roulade

serves 4

2 tablespoons olive oil

2 large leeks, washed and sliced into rings

300 g waxy potatoes

freshly ground black pepper

200 g low-fat ricotta cheese

1 tablespoon plain, low-fat yoghurt

1 omega-enriched egg, beaten

2 tablespoons chopped chives

2 tablespoons chopped fresh dill

300 g seafood (combination of peeled and deveined green
  prawns, scallops and firm fish fillets, cut into small cubes)

6 sheets filo pastry

oil spray

milk to brush on pastry

1 Preheat oven to 200°C. Heat oil in a non-stick frypan and cook leeks for 3-4 minutes over a gentle heat until soft. Parboil potatoes until still firm. Drain, season well with pepper, then cube.

2 Mix together ricotta cheese, yoghurt, egg, chives, dill and pepper to taste. Add leeks, potato and seafood and combine.

3 Cover a flat baking tray with oven-bake paper. Spread over a sheet of filo pastry and spray with oil spray. Repeat with remaining 5 sheets. Spoon seafood filling onto the filo pastry, about ⅓ of the way down pastry sheet. Fold in the ends of the filo and gently roll up to make a roulade. Brush top with a little milk.

4 Bake for 30 minutes until brown. Serve with fresh salad or steamed greens.

GLYCAEMIC LOAD ¾

Per serve	
Energy	1530 kJ
Protein	25 g
Fat	21 g
Carbohydrate	17 g
Fibre	4 g
GI	Medium

grilled tandoori beef kebabs with spicy smashed sweet potatoes

serves 4

400 g lean rump steak, cut into medium chunks
1 tablespoon tandoori spice paste
1 tablespoon white vinegar
500 g sweet potatoes, washed and cut into chunks
1 tablespoon canola oil
1 teaspoon black mustard seeds
½ teaspoon ground turmeric
1 small green chilli, roughly chopped
¾ cup low-fat coconut milk
2 tablespoons lime or lemon juice
freshly ground black pepper
2 tablespoons coriander leaves for garnish

1 Mix beef with tandoori spice and vinegar and marinate for 1 hour. Skewer onto metal kebab sticks and put aside.

2 Cook sweet potatoes in boiling water until just tender. Drain and put aside.

3 In a saucepan, heat oil and cook mustard seeds for 1-2 minutes over a high heat until they pop. Stir in turmeric, chilli and coconut milk. Bring to the boil then add the sweet potatoes and cook for 4-5 minutes. Gently 'smash' the sweet potatoes with a potato masher. Season with lime juice and black pepper.

4 Preheat grill or barbecue and cook kebabs over a high heat for 2-3 minutes each side until lightly browned and done. Serve immediately with potatoes garnished with coriander leaves.

GLYCAEMIC LOAD ¾

Per serve	
Energy	1400 kJ
Protein	24 g
Fat	16 g
Carbohydrate	23 g
Fibre	4 g
GI	Low

greek feta
and potato filo pie

Serves 6 – 8

2 tablespoons virgin olive oil

2 large onions, peeled and sliced into rings

400 g potatoes (2 medium), peeled

400 g sweet potato (1 medium), peeled

150 g Greek feta cheese, roughly chopped

3 teaspoons dried tarragon or
   ½ cup fresh chopped tarragon leaves

2 tablespoons finely chopped parsley

1 cup diced fresh tomatoes or canned chopped tomatoes

black pepper

6 sheets filo pastry

1 tablespoon sesame seeds

1 Preheat oven to 200°C. Heat oil in a non-stick frypan and cook onion slowly until browned. Put aside.

2 Steam potatoes and sweet potato until almost cooked. Remove from steamer, cool, then cut into small chunks. Mix together onion, potatoes, feta cheese, tarragon, parsley and tomatoes and season with pepper.

3 Lightly oil a 20 cm square ceramic pie dish and line with 4 sheets filo pastry, lightly spraying the top of each sheet with oil. Add potato mix then cover with a sheet of filo pastry. Spray with oil then top with remaining sheet of filo pastry. Sprinkle with sesame seeds to finish.

4 Bake for 20-25 minutes until lightly browned. Serve while warm, accompanied with a crisp green salad.

> **Winning tip**
> *Filo is extremely low in fat, which makes it a great alternative to mainstream pastries.*

GLYCAEMIC LOAD 1½

Per serve	
Energy	1570 kJ
Protein	17 g
Fat	16 g
Carbohydrate	37 g
Fibre	6 g
GI	Medium

spanish tortilla
with avocado, tomato
and onion salad

serves 4

6 potatoes (good boiling ones like Roseval,
    Kipfler, Nicola, Desiree)
4 onions, peeled and thinly sliced
1 leek, washed and sliced
125 ml water or vegetable stock
6 green onions, chopped
8 omega-enriched eggs
2 tablespoons crème fraîche
good pinch of ground nutmeg
¼ teaspoon ground black pepper
1 tablespoon chopped fresh chives

Salad
4 tomatoes, thinly sliced
1 red onion, thinly sliced
1 small, firm ripe avocado
1 tablespoon lemon juice
2 tablespoons olive oil

1 Preheat oven to 180°C. Place potatoes in a large pot
  of water and slowly bring to the boil. Cook until tender,
  then cool. Peel skins and chop into small chunks.
2 Place onion and water in a saucepan and cook over
  a medium heat, stirring occasionally until onion is soft,
  about 10 minutes. Stir in leek and cook for a further
  10 minutes. Remove from heat and stir in spring onion.
3 Line a 3 cm x 18 cm x 28 cm baking dish with oven-bake
  paper. Spread potatoes over the bottom of the dish
  then spread over the cooked onion mixture.
4 Beat together eggs, crème fraîche, nutmeg and pepper.
  Pour over potato and onions then sprinkle with
  chopped chives. Bake for 25-30 minutes until eggs
  are set. Remove from oven, cool slightly then slice.
5 To prepare salad, place tomatoes and onions in a bowl.
  Dice avocado and stir through. Dress with lemon juice
  and olive oil. Serve a little on the side of the tortilla.

GLYCAEMIC LOAD 1½

Per serve	
Energy	2030 kJ
Protein	22 g
Fat	26 g
Carbohydrate	35 g
Fibre	9 g
GI	Medium

silverbeet, potato and herb bake

serves 4 – 6

1 bunch silverbeet (10 stems)
500 g waxy potatoes, washed
250 g low-fat ricotta cheese
2 tablespoons grated Parmesan cheese
2 omega-enriched eggs
100 ml buttermilk
2 tablespoons chopped parsley
2 tablespoons chopped lemon thyme
1 teaspoon ground nutmeg
black pepper to season
1 tablespoon roasted flaked almonds

1 Preheat oven to 180°C. Discard all but the green part of the silverbeet. Wash well and drain. Place in a large pot of boiling water, cover and cook for 1 minute until wilted. Drain and squeeze out any excess water. Chop roughly.

2 Steam potatoes until soft. Cool then cut into thin slices. Put ricotta cheese, Parmesan cheese, eggs, buttermilk, parsley, thyme, nutmeg and pepper into a food processor and blend well.

3 Grease or spray with oil a large baking dish (about 20 cm x 28 cm). Put in a layer of potatoes, top with half the silverbeet then add half the cheese mixture. Repeat, ending with layer of cheese mixture. Sprinkle with flaked almonds and bake for around 30 minutes until golden brown.

GLYCAEMIC LOAD ½

Per serve	
Energy	1060 kJ
Protein	17 g
Fat	11 g
Carbohydrate	19 g
Fibre	5 g
GI	Medium

rich vegetable casserole with spicy tofu

serves 4

1 tablespoon virgin olive oil

1 large onion, finely chopped

2 cloves garlic, finely chopped

300 ml vegetable stock

1 large sweet potato, peeled and cut into cubes (about 400 g)

2 carrots, peeled and cut into chunks

2 parsnips, peeled and cut into chunks

1 swede, peeled and cut into chunks

¼ cup crunchy peanut butter

100 g spicy marinated tofu, cut into small chunks

1 cup Doongara rice, boiled, to serve

1 Heat oil in a large saucepan and cook onion and garlic over a low heat until translucent. Pour in stock and bring to the boil. Add sweet potato, carrot, parsnip and swede and simmer for 15 minutes.

2 Ladle about 1 cup of hot broth into a bowl. Transfer to a food processor, add peanut butter and blend. Pour the mixture back into the saucepan and add marinated tofu. Cook for 5 minutes to heat through the tofu.

3 To serve, prepare deep bowls of boiled Doongara rice – to make up carbohydrate – and spoon over the casserole.

GLYCAEMIC LOAD 1

Per serve (without rice)	
Energy	1450 kJ
Protein	14 g
Fat	16 g
Carbohydrate	30 g
Fibre	10 g
GI	Low

spicy chicken and sweet potato baked in paper

serves 4

500 g chicken tenderloins
2 sweet potatoes, peeled and thinly sliced (about 500 g)
4 x 40 cm squares oven-bake paper
parsley or coriander sprigs for garnish

Spice mixture
2 teaspoons grated fresh ginger
1 clove garlic, crushed
¼ teaspoon crushed dried chilli
1 tablespoon chopped fresh parsley
¼ teaspoon cumin seeds
⅓ cup low-fat coconut milk

1 Preheat oven to 180°C. To prepare spice mixture, combine all ingredients and mix well. Coat chicken with spice mixture.
2 Arrange a quarter of the sweet potato in overlapping slices on one square of paper and spoon over a quarter of the chicken mixture. Close the parcel and seal well by folding and pinching edges. Repeat with the remaining three portions of chicken and sweet potato.
3 Place parcels on an oven tray and bake for about 20-25 minutes until chicken and sweet potato is cooked. To serve, open the top of each parcel and decorate with coriander or parsley sprigs. Accompany with stir-fried Asian greens.

GLYCAEMIC LOAD ½

Per serve	
Energy	1160 kJ
Protein	28 g
Fat	8 g
Carbohydrate	20 g
Fibre	7 g
GI	Low

marinated pork chops with roasted pear and sweet potato

serves 4

4 pork chops (about 150-175 g each), trimmed of fat
2 tablespoons lemon juice
1 tablespoon coarse grain mustard
1 tablespoon fresh sage leaves, torn
4 pears
500 g sweet potato
2 tablespoons virgin olive oil
black pepper

1 Preheat oven to 200°C. Place chops in a bowl. Coat well with lemon juice, mustard and sage leaves and leave to marinate.
2 Wash, quarter and core pears. Wash sweet potato and cut into chunks, the same size as the pear quarters. Toss pears and potatoes in oil and pepper. Place on a baking tray and cook for about 20 minutes, tossing once during the cooking.
3 Add marinated chops and continue cooking for a further 20 minutes, or until chops are cooked through. Serve immediately with extra coarse grain mustard on the side and steamed green vegetables.

GLYCAEMIC LOAD 1

Per serve	
Energy	1690 kJ
Protein	27 g
Fat	14 g
Carbohydrate	41 g
Fibre	7 g
GI	Low

creamy lemon and chive potato salad with honey leg ham

serves 4

200 g sweet potatoes, washed and cut into chunks
200 g waxy potatoes, washed and cut into chunks
200 g honey leg ham, finely shredded
1 handful mixed salad leaves

Dressing
1 tablespoon fresh lemon juice
2 teaspoons freshly grated lemon rind
1 cup silken tofu, drained
2 tablespoons roughly chopped fresh chives
1 tablespoon Dijon mustard
1 tablespoon white wine vinegar
ground black pepper

1 Cook potatoes in boiling water until tender. Drain and cool.
2 Place all dressing ingredients in a food processor and process until smooth and creamy.
3 Pour dressing over potatoes and mix, then stir through the ham. Serve spooned over a few mixed salad leaves.

GLYCAEMIC LOAD ¾

Per serve	
Energy	810 kJ
Protein	27 g
Fat	6 g
Carbohydrate	14 g
Fibre	3 g
GI	Medium

veal schnitzels with potato and caramelised onion bake

serves 4

500 g potatoes, peeled and sliced
500 g sweet potato, peeled and sliced
1 tablespoon virgin olive oil
2 medium onions, peeled and thinly sliced
1 garlic clove, crushed
2 sprigs fresh rosemary leaves
2 sprigs fresh thyme leaves
salt
freshly ground black pepper
½ cup freshly grated Parmesan cheese
2 large eggs
¾ cup skim milk
pinch of ground nutmeg
8 veal schnitzels (approximately 480 g)

1 Preheat oven to 170°C. Steam potatoes until just tender. Cool and put aside.

2 Heat oil in a heavy non-stick frypan and cook onion over a medium heat for 5 minutes, stirring occasionally. Reduce heat and cook for a further 15 minutes until onions begin to brown. Stir in garlic, rosemary and fresh thyme leaves. Cool and put aside.

3 Lightly grease a shallow baking dish. Cover base with half of the potatoes, overlapping them slightly. Season with salt and pepper. Top with the onions and half of the Parmesan cheese. Cover with remaining potato slices.

4 Beat together eggs and skim milk and stir in nutmeg. Pour over potatoes and sprinkle with remaining Parmesan cheese. Bake for about 45 minutes until custard has set and top is golden.

5 To cook veal, spray a non-stick frypan with a little more oil and sauté schnitzels for a few minutes on each side. Serve a wedge of the potato dish with the veal schnitzels and accompany with steamed green vegetables or a mixed leaf salad.

GLYCAEMIC LOAD 1½

Per serve	
Energy	1990 kJ
Protein	44 g
Fat	14 g
Carbohydrate	40 g
Fibre	6 g
GI	Medium

grilled lamb cutlets with smashed minted peas and potatoes

serves 4

400 g potatoes, quartered
1 tablespoon virgin olive oil
½ cup buttermilk
8 trim baby lamb cutlets (approximately 480 g)
freshly ground black pepper
200 g fresh, frozen or canned peas
1 teaspoon white wine vinegar
½ cup fresh mint leaves

1 Cook potatoes in salted water until tender. Gently smash with a potato masher and stir in oil and buttermilk. Transfer to an ovenproof dish, cover with foil and place in oven to keep warm.
2 Preheat a char-grill pan over a high heat. Season cutlets with pepper and brush a little oil over each side. Cook cutlets in batches for 3-4 minutes each side, depending on the thickness.
3 Cook peas until tender and purée with vinegar and fresh mint leaves. Stir into cooked potatoes. To serve, place a spoonful of potato in centre of each plate and top with a grilled lamb cutlet. Accompany with steamed greens or carrots.

GLYCAEMIC LOAD 1

Per serve	
Energy	1100 kJ
Protein	22 g
Fat	12 g
Carbohydrate	19 g
Fibre	6 g
GI	Low

lamb pie with spicy potato topping

serves 4

400 g floury potatoes, peeled and cut into chunks
400 g sweet potatoes, peeled and cut into chunks
4 tablespoons low-fat milk
1 tablespoon coarse-grain honey mustard
1 teaspoon virgin olive oil
450 g lean minced lamb
1 teaspoon oregano
1 onion, finely chopped
2 stalks celery, finely chopped
1 medium carrot, diced
2 tomatoes, roughly chopped
½ cup chicken, beef or vegetable stock
2 tablespoons cornflour, mixed with 1 tablespoon water
1 tablespoon worcestershire sauce

1 Preheat oven to 200°C. Cook potatoes in boiling water until tender. Drain and mash with milk and seeded mustard. Put aside.
2 In a large saucepan, heat oil and cook lamb until lightly browned. Stir in oregano, onion, celery, carrots and tomatoes and cook for 4-5 minutes. Combine stock, cornflour and worcestershire sauce and stir into lamb mixture. Bring to the boil and cook for 3-4 minutes.
3 Transfer lamb mixture to a large ovenproof dish. Top with mashed potato. Draw curved lines in potato with tines of fork – potato will brown and crisp along the lines.
4 Bake for 30-35 minutes, until topping has browned. Serve immediately with steamed green vegetables or salad.

GLYCAEMIC LOAD 1¾

Per serve	
Energy	1600 kJ
Protein	31 g
Fat	9 g
Carbohydrate	41 g
Fibre	7 g
GI	Low

rice

Did you know that rice just about trebles in weight during cooking? So 50 g per person of raw rice will give you approximately 150 g per person of cooked rice, which is roughly one of our load servings.

The range of rice types available is extensive with some rice being grown specifically for particular types of cooking methods and recipes. Brown rice has the bran layer still intact, which adds a nutty taste. White rice is the polished grain with the bran layer removed. Although there is more fibre in brown rice it does not necessarily have a low GI. Wild rice (not really a rice, but an aquatic grass) can be used in pilaf, salads, plain or boiled. We think this has a medium GI.

What we feature in our recipes are the low glycaemic types – Basmati and Doongara rice – and we have adapted these to suit all the different cooking methods.

Whatever rice you use, we suggest you store it in an airtight container.

Cooking rice

Instructions follow for the two most basic ways to cook rice. The rice packet will normally give you cooking instructions, but often this will be thrown out.

Simple absorption method for rice

Serves 4

1 cup rice (measured to 250 ml)
2 cups water (measured to 500 ml)
salt

1 Place rice and water in a saucepan and add a pinch of salt. Cover the pan with a tight-fitting lid and bring to the boil over a high heat.
2 Once boiling, immediately reduce the heat to low and cook for 15 minutes. Do not lift the lid at any time. Remove from the heat and stand, still covered, for 10 minutes.
3 Fluff up rice with a fork and serve immediately.

> *Winning tip*
> *Remember, if you measure the rice in the same cup in which you measure the water, you can't go wrong.*

Rapid boil method

Serves 4

8 cups water (2 litres)
1 cup rice (250 ml)

1 Pour water into a saucepan, cover with a lid and bring to the boil. Pour in the rice and bring back to the boil.
2 Cook, uncovered, for 10-15 minutes. Drain in a strainer immediately and serve.

> *Winning tip*
> *Rice is easy to cook in a microwave oven. For the cooking time and liquid required, refer to the cooking instructions for your microwave.*

contents

mulligatawny soup

serves 4

2 tablespoons virgin olive oil

1 onion, peeled and finely chopped

1 carrot, peeled and finely chopped

1 stalk celery, finely chopped

1 small green capsicum, de-seeded and finely chopped

2 tablespoons plain flour

1 tablespoon Madras curry powder

4 cups chicken stock

3 cloves

1 cinnamon stick

4 cardamom pods

3 tomatoes, roughly chopped

250 g chicken thigh fillets, cut into thin shreds

1½ cups cooked Basmati rice

1 Heat oil in a saucepan and add onion, carrot, celery and green capsicum. Cook over a gentle heat until soft. Stir in flour and curry powder and cook for 2-3 minutes.

2 Slowly pour in stock then add cloves, cinnamon stick, cardamom pods and tomatoes. Bring to the boil and simmer for 40 minutes. Stir in chicken and cook for a further 10 minutes.

3 Stir in cooked rice and heat through for 5 minutes. Serve immediately.

GLYCAEMIC LOAD 1

Per serve	
Energy	1400 kJ
Protein	20 g
Fat	14 g
Carbohydrate	30 g
Fibre	3 g
GI	Low

greek chicken and lemon soup

serves 4

50 g Doongara rice
juice of 1 lemon
3 omega-enriched eggs, beaten
5 cups chicken stock
50 g cooked chicken meat, shredded
salt
freshly ground black pepper
2 tablespoons finely chopped parsley for garnish

1 Cook rice for 15-20 minutes in boiling salted water until just tender, then drain. In a bowl, lightly whisk lemon juice and eggs until well combined.
2 Heat chicken stock in a saucepan. Remove about 250 ml of the hot stock and, a little at a time, whisk into eggs and lemon juice until combined.
3 Remove chicken stock from heat and slowly whisk in the egg mixture. Stir in cooked rice and chicken and cook over a low heat for 5 minutes, being careful not to let the soup boil.
4 Season to taste with salt and pepper, ladle into soup bowls and garnish with parsley.

GLYCAEMIC LOAD ½

Per serve	
Energy	650 kJ
Protein	12 g
Fat	6 g
Carbohydrate	12 g
Fibre	1 g
GI	Low

marinated tofu and sautéed asian greens on steamed basmati rice

serves 4

1 tablespoon virgin olive oil

2 tablespoons red wine vinegar

1 tablespoon finely chopped garlic

1 bunch broccolini or 2 cups broccoli florets

6 baby bok choy, cut in half lengthways and washed thoroughly

1 bunch English spinach, washed, stalks removed and shredded

2 blocks of marinated firm tofu (600 g), chopped into cubes

1 tablespoon toasted sesame seeds

ground black pepper

2 cups cooked Basmati rice

1 Place a large wok over a high heat and add oil, vinegar, garlic and broccolini. Pour in ⅓ cup of water and stir. Cover and cook until all liquid has evaporated. Remove to a bowl.

2 Cook bok choy and spinach, stir-frying until just beginning to wilt. Stir in chopped tofu to heat through then return garlic and broccolini to wok.

3 Stir in toasted sesame seeds and serve immediately in bowls of steaming hot Basmati rice.

GLYCAEMIC LOAD 1¾

Per serve	
Energy	1910 kJ
Protein	28 g
Fat	16 g
Carbohydrate	44 g
Fibre	9 g
GI	Low

grilled vegetable rice tart

serves 4

1 cup Doongara rice

2 cups vegetable stock

1 zucchini, thinly sliced lengthways

1 small eggplant, cut in half and thinly sliced lengthways

1 small red capsicum, de-seeded and thinly sliced

2 tablespoons virgin olive oil

freshly ground black pepper

2 omega-enriched eggs

1 tablespoon freshly chopped Italian parsley

1 cup tomato pasta sauce

1 tablespoon finely grated Parmesan cheese

mixed salad leaves, to serve

1 Preheat oven to 190°C. Cook rice in stock until tender, using the absorption method (*see* page 49). Remove to a bowl and cool.

2 Heat a char-grill pan and cook zucchini, eggplant and capsicum for 2-3 minutes each side. Toss with a little oil and season with pepper.

3 Mix eggs and parsley and stir through the cooled rice. Season to taste with freshly ground black pepper. Spoon into a lightly oiled flan tin (about 23 cm diameter), pressing the mixture down to form a base.

4 Spread pasta sauce over the rice and top with the char-grilled zucchini, eggplant and capsicum. Sprinkle with Parmesan cheese and bake for 20-25 minutes until vegetables are soft and cheese is melted and lightly browned. Serve hot.

GLYCAEMIC LOAD 1¾

Per serve	
Energy	1500 kJ
Protein	11 g
Fat	14 g
Carbohydrate	46 g
Fibre	3 g
GI	Low

indian cashew nut and vegetable curry

serves 4

150 g raw cashew nuts
1 tablespoon vegetable oil
1 tablespoon freshly grated ginger
½ teaspoon ground turmeric
1 teaspoon ground cumin
1 teaspoon ground coriander
½ teaspoon chilli paste
2 cups vegetable stock
1 large carrot cut into small cubes
4 spring onions quartered and cut into 5 cm sticks
200 g green beans, topped and tailed and cut into 5 cm pieces
1 large zucchini, cut into 5 cm sticks
salt and black pepper (optional)
2 tablespoons chilled light coconut milk
2 cups Basmati rice, cooked

1 Place cashew nuts in a bowl, cover with water and leave to soak for 30 minutes.
2 Heat oil in a saucepan and fry ginger, turmeric, cumin, coriander and chilli paste for 2 minutes. Add stock, carrots and drained cashew nuts and simmer for 5 minutes. Add spring onions, beans, and zucchini and simmer, covered, for a further 10 minutes until vegetables and cashew nuts are tender.
3 Season, if desired. Serve over plates of steaming hot Basmati rice and garnish with chilled light coconut milk.

> **Winning tip**
> This is a higher-fat recipe that contains many of the essential fats plus important vitamin E. The fact that the per-serve fat count is high compared to some recipes does not discount this dish. We recommend serving it with a second, lighter curry. That will halve the portion size and, therefore, reduce the fat intake for the meal.

GLYCAEMIC LOAD 1¼

Per serve	
Energy	1810 kJ
Protein	12 g
Fat	24 g
Carbohydrate	38 g
Fibre	6 g
GI	Low

vietnamese-style rice paper roll-ups

serves 4

50 g dried rice vermicelli, soaked in hot water for
   10 minutes then drained
1 cup fresh bean sprouts
¼ cup fresh mint leaves
¼ cup finely chopped roasted peanuts
1 tablespoon chopped coriander leaves
2 spring onions, cut into thin long strips
1 small carrot, peeled and finely grated
¼ cup shredded iceberg lettuce
1 tablespoon sweet soy sauce
1 tablespoon lemon juice
12 medium-sized rice papers

Sweet Soy and Chilli Dipping Sauce
¼ cup sweet soy sauce
2 tablespoons fresh lemon juice
1 tablespoon sweet chilli sauce or hot chilli sauce
1 tablespoon finely chopped roasted peanuts

1 In a large bowl, mix vermicelli, bean sprouts, mint leaves, roasted peanuts, coriander leaves, spring onions, carrot, lettuce, sweet soy sauce and lemon juice until well combined.

2 Fill a shallow bowl with hot water. Dip a rice paper sheet into the water until it is soft and flexible. Transfer to a dampened sheet of oven-bake paper.

3 Spoon 1-2 tablespoons of filling into the centre of the sheet. Fold in three sides then roll up tightly to make a small log. Put on a platter and cover with a damp kitchen towel. Repeat the procedure until all the filling has been used.

4 To prepare dipping sauce, place sweet soy sauce, lemon juice, chilli sauce and peanuts in a bowl. Stir until well combined. Serve with the roll-ups.

GLYCAEMIC LOAD ¼

Per serve	
Energy	400 kJ
Protein	4 g
Fat	5 g
Carbohydrate	7 g
Fibre	2 g
GI	Low

mushroom, leek and pinenut frittata

serves 4

¾ cup Doongara rice
1½ cups chicken stock
1 tablespoon virgin olive oil
1 onion, finely chopped
300 g field or Swiss brown mushrooms, roughly chopped
1 clove garlic, finely chopped
½ cup toasted wholegrain breadcrumbs
¼ cup flaked almonds, toasted
½ cup finely grated Parmesan cheese
3 omega-enriched eggs

1 Preheat oven to 180°C. Place rice and stock in a saucepan and bring to the boil. Cover and reduce heat to a low simmer for 10 minutes, turn off heat and stand for 10 minutes.
2 Heat oil in a frypan and cook onion over a low heat until soft. Add mushrooms and garlic and cook for 3-4 minutes, until mushrooms have softened. Remove from the heat then mix in breadcrumbs, almonds, Parmesan and rice. Whisk together the eggs and pour into the mushroom mixture.
3 Line the base of a 20 cm spring-form cake tin with oven-bake paper. Pour in rice and mushroom mixture. Bake for 35-45 minutes, until set.
4 Remove from oven and cool a little before cutting into wedges. Serve with a mixed leaf salad.

> **Winning tip**
> When making frittata with a vegetable that has a high water content, like mushrooms, adding toasted wholegrain breadcrumbs helps to absorb moisture and also adds flavour and texture. Swiss brown mushrooms have a delicious nutty flavour that complements the nuttiness of the bread.

GLYCAEMIC LOAD 1½

Per serve	
Energy	1520 kJ
Protein	16 g
Fat	15 g
Carbohydrate	40 g
Fibre	4 g
GI	Low

rice-stuffed tomatoes with tuna and basil

serves 4

8 medium-sized firm tomatoes
freshly ground black pepper
1 tablespoon virgin olive oil
3 spring onions, roughly chopped
1 garlic clove, crushed
1½ cups cooked Doongara rice
2 tablespoons tomato juice
2 teaspoons lemon juice
100 g tuna, drained and flaked
200 pimento stuffed green olives, roughly chopped
¼ cup finely chopped fresh basil
mixed salad leaves to serve

1 Cut tops off tomatoes and put aside. Carefully scoop out seeds and discard flesh. Season tomato cups with pepper then place upside down on kitchen paper. Leave to drain for 10 minutes.
2 Heat oil in a non-stick frypan and cook spring onions and garlic over a low heat until soft. Remove from heat and stir into the cooked rice. Stir in tomato juice, lemon juice, tuna, olives, basil and pepper to taste.
3 Stuff tomatoes with rice mixture and replace tops. Serve at room temperature with a handful of mixed salad leaves.

Winning tip
Cooked, peeled school prawns can be mixed into the rice instead of tuna. By mistake, the first time we calculated this recipe we used regular high-GI rice. The result? Same energy, same amount of carbohydrate but the Glycaemic Load was 1½ times that of this dish cooked with the Doongara rice. Seeking out the lower-GI foods can definitely make a big glycaemic impact.

GLYCAEMIC LOAD 1

Per serve	
Energy	1110 kJ
Protein	11 g
Fat	10 g
Carbohydrate	28 g
Fibre	9 g
GI	Low

smoked salmon and leek risotto

serves 4

2 tablespoons virgin olive oil

2 leeks, washed and roughly chopped

2 cloves garlic, finely chopped

1 cup Doongara Rice

1 cup white wine

1½ litres fish or vegetable stock

150 g smoked salmon, roughly chopped

2 tablespoons light sour cream

1 tablespoon chopped fresh dill

salt

freshly ground black pepper

3 tablespoons lemon zest

1 Heat oil in a large saucepan and cook leeks slowly until soft. Add garlic and cook for 2-3 minutes. Stir in rice and cook for 2-3 minutes. Pour in wine and bring to the boil, stirring continuously.

2 In another saucepan, heat stock to a simmer. Slowly add stock to rice, 3-4 tablespoons at a time, ensuring stock is slowly absorbed after each addition.

3 When rice is tender and creamy, stir in smoked salmon, sour cream and dill. Season with salt and pepper. Cover and stand for 3 minutes. Serve in shallow bowls and garnish with lemon zest.

Winning tip
The secret to a good risotto is to avoid using too much liquid too quickly – add it slowly, stirring constantly until you have creamy rice. Risotto can be flavoured with many different ingredients. Use the first 6 ingredients in our recipe as a base then stir in chopped sautéed mushrooms, roasted beetroot or pumpkin, or whatever you wish to try. Give a vegetable risotto a flourish by adding a little grated Parmesan cheese and fresh chopped herbs at the end.

GLYCAEMIC LOAD 1¾

Per serve	
Energy	1840 kJ
Protein	18 g
Fat	15 g
Carbohydrate	46 g
Fibre	2 g
GI	Low

baked fish with spicy vegetable rice

serves 4

2 tablespoons vegetable oil, plus extra to coat fish

2 cinnamon sticks, broken

4 bay leaves, broken

½ teaspoon whole cumin seeds

1 onion, finely chopped

6 whole cloves

pinch of ground turmeric

1 cup green peas

½ cup finely chopped carrots

1 cup Basmati rice

½ cup boiling water or chicken or vegetable stock

4 fish fillets (200 g each) (blue eye, snapper fillets or similar)

lemon wedges for garnish

1 Preheat oven to 180°C. Heat oil in a large saucepan, add cinnamon, bay leaves and cumin seeds and sauté for 1-2 minutes. Add onion, cloves and turmeric and continue cooking until onion is golden and coated with the spices.

2 Stir in peas and carrots. Add rice and cook for about 1 minute. Pour in boiling water. Bring mixture to the boil, stirring several times. Reduce heat to the lowest setting and cover. Cook until water has evaporated, about 20 minutes or longer. Turn off heat and stand for 10 minutes.

3 Brush fish fillets with oil and season with black pepper. Arrange on a baking tray lined with oven-bake paper and cook for 5-10 minutes until cooked through. Serve with spicy vegetable rice and garnish with lemon wedges.

GLYCAEMIC LOAD 1¾

Per serve	
Energy	2070 kJ
Protein	47 g
Fat	13 g
Carbohydrate	46 g
Fibre	3 g
GI	Low

grilled fish steaks with green rice

serves 4

½ cup coriander leaves
1 cup English spinach leaves, washed and stalks removed
1 cup chicken or vegetable stock
1 cup low-fat milk
2 tablespoons virgin olive oil plus extra to coat fish
1 cup Doongara rice
1 small onion, finely chopped
1 garlic clove, finely chopped
4 fish steaks (blue eye, Atlantic salmon, kingfish)

1 Place coriander leaves, spinach and stock in a blender and purée. Add milk and blend until well combined.
2 Heat oil in a saucepan, stir in rice, onion and garlic and cook for 2-3 minutes. Add blended vegetables and slowly bring to the boil. Cover pan and reduce heat to a very low simmer. Cook for 20 minutes, then turn off the heat and stand for 10 minutes.
3 Brush fish steaks with a little virgin olive oil and grill for 3-4 minutes each side until cooked. Serve on the rice with lemon wedges as garnish.

Winning tip
This recipe is inspired by a Mexican rice dish that introduces all kinds of flavours when cooking rice by the absorption method. Here we add coriander and spinach, but substituting puréed tomatoes and grilled red capsicums will inject a pink blush to the rice.

GLYCAEMIC LOAD 1¾

Per serve	
Energy	1810 kJ
Protein	35 g
Fat	16 g
Carbohydrate	47 g
Fibre	2 g
GI	Low

baked spicy chicken with rice pilaf

serves 4

1 teaspoon ground sweet paprika
¼ teaspoon ground hot paprika
1 tablespoon plain low-fat yoghurt
4 chicken thighs, skin removed
2 tablespoons light olive oil
1 medium onion, finely chopped
1 cup Doongara rice
¼ cup raisins
good pinch of saffron threads infused in ¼ cup of hot water
1½ cups stock (vegetable, chicken or beef) or water
2 tablespoons roasted almonds
¼ cup chopped fresh mint leaves

1 Preheat oven to 200°C. Combine spices and yoghurt and smear over chicken. Bake in oven for about 15 minutes until cooked through.
2 In a heavy saucepan, heat oil and cook onion for 3-4 minutes, until soft. Stir in rice and cook for 2-3 minutes, stirring continuously. Add raisins, saffron and stock and bring to the boil. Cover pan tightly and reduce heat. Simmer for 20 minutes.
3 Remove from heat and stand for 5 minutes. Remove lid and fluff up rice with a fork. Stir in almonds and fresh mint leaves. Spoon onto plates, top with chicken and serve immediately.

> **Winning tip**
> Pilaf is gloriously versatile. At the start of the cooking, when frying the onion and rice, you can add all manner of spices and flavourings, including fresh ingredients like ginger and garlic and whole spices like cumin, coriander, cinnamon sticks and cardamom seeds. Cooking the rice with stock lends extra richness and flavour. Basmati or Doongara rice work well with this style of rice dish.

GLYCAEMIC LOAD 2

Per serve	
Energy	2150 kJ
Protein	29 g
Fat	21 g
Carbohydrate	50 g
Fibre	9 g
GI	Medium

moroccan lamb with rice pilaf

serves 6

1 kg lean cubed lamb, trimmed of all visible fat

1 tablespoon olive oil

1 teaspoon finely grated ginger

pinch of saffron threads (optional)

salt

freshly ground black pepper

½ teaspoon ground coriander

1 teaspoon ground cinnamon

1 large onion, finely chopped

100 g dried prunes, pitted and roughly chopped

1 bunch English spinach, stalks removed, washed and chopped

1 cup Doongara rice

2 tablespoons roasted sesame seeds for garnish

1 Place lamb, oil, ginger, saffron (if using), salt, pepper, coriander, cinnamon and onion in a large saucepan. Cover with approximately 1½ litres of water, bring to the boil then cover and simmer gently for about 1-1½ hours, until lamb is tender.

2 Add prunes and cook for 20 minutes. Stir in spinach, cook for a further 5 minutes, then taste and adjust seasoning if necessary.

3 To prepare pilaf, bring stock to the boil, stir in rice and return to the boil. Cover and cook over a low heat for 12 minutes. Turn off heat, cover and stand for 10 minutes. Garnish rice pilaf with toasted sesame seeds, spoon over the lamb and serve.

Winning tip
Although it is quick to prepare, the flavours develop gradually in this slow-cooking recipe. The result is a rich, delicious dish that is fit for a sultan's table.

GLYCAEMIC LOAD 1¼

Per serve	
Energy	1800 kJ
Protein	41 g
Fat	16 g
Carbohydrate	36 g
Fibre	4 g
GI	Low

thai-style beef salad

serves 4

400 g lean minced beef

3 tablespoons of water

1 teaspoon rice flour, mixed with 1 tablespoon of water

1 tablespoon of lemon juice

½ tablespoon of fish sauce

1 large red onion sliced thinly, quartered and thinly sliced

1 tablespoon chopped green onions

2 tablespoons fresh mint leaves, roughly chopped

2 tablespoons fresh coriander leaves

1 large carrot, finely grated

200 g rice vermicelli noodles, soaked in boiling water until soft

8 small leaves of iceberg lettuce, washed

1 In a wok or frypan cook beef in water until medium-rare. Stir in rice flour and water mixture and cook for about 2 minutes until thickened.

2 Transfer beef to a bowl with lemon juice, fish sauce, red onion and green onions. Cool completely before adding chopped mint, coriander leaves and grated carrot. Mix well. Stir in rice noodles, spoon into lettuce cups and serve immediately.

GLYCAEMIC LOAD ½

Per serve	
Energy	950 kJ
Protein	23 g
Fat	7 g
Carbohydrate	16 g
Fibre	3 g
GI	Low

pasta

We believe that one reason pasta is so popular is because of its low GI – which explains why most pasta meals are filling and satisfying.

You can buy pasta dried or fresh, long, short, flat and stuffed or filled. Some common types of pasta are tagliatelle, taglierini, spaghetti, capelli d'angelo, fusilli, farfalle, rigatoni, penne, macaroni, fettuccine, cannelloni, lasagne, linguine, vermicelli and pappardelle. The stuffed varieties are tortellini, ravioli and agnolotti.

Pasta is made from durum wheat flour, which is also known as semolina. Pasta's other key ingredient is milk. Some of the fresh pastas have added ingredients, such as egg, vegetables and other interesting flavourings.

Fresh pasta will keep for 2-3 days stored in an airtight container in the fridge. Alternatively it can be stored in the freezer.

Cooking pasta

Bring a large saucepan of water to the boil and add 2-3 teaspoons of salt. If you cook your pasta in plenty of boiling water, it will not stick together. It is not necessary to add oil to the water.

Add the pasta to the pot of boiling water, return it to the boil and cook as follows:

3-4 minutes for fresh pasta
10-15 minutes for dried pasta
8-10 minutes for fresh filled pasta
15-20 minutes for dried filled pasta

Here are some helpful hints for cooking pasta:

- When cooking long pasta, like spaghetti, hold it at the end and slowly push it into the boiling water. The pasta will soften and will eventually fit into the saucepan without breaking.

- Always test your pasta before draining it to make sure it has lost the raw flour taste and still has some elasticity. It should not be soft or start to fall apart.

- Remove cooked filled pasta like ravioli or tortellini from the saucepan with a large, flat, slotted spoon or skimmer. This will prevent it from splitting.

- Toss drained, cooked pasta with a little virgin olive oil to stop it from sticking together and to add flavour.

- To re-heat cooked pasta, place in a colander or sieve and lower into a pot of boiling water for 2-3 minutes, until it has heated through.

contents

hot smoked atlantic salmon and pasta bake

serves 4

350 g dried pasta (farfalle, fussilli, orecchlette)
200 g hot smoked Atlantic salmon or ocean trout, flaked
200 g ricotta cheese
2 tablespoons low-fat milk
zest of 1 lemon, finely grated
3 tablespoons chopped fresh basil
4 tablespoons grated fresh Parmesan cheese

1 Preheat oven to 180°C. Cook pasta and cool. Place half in the bottom of a small shallow baking dish then top with flaked salmon.

2 In a bowl, mix ricotta cheese, milk, lemon zest and basil. Spread half this mixture over the layer of flaked salmon. Cover with remainder of pasta then top with remaining ricotta. Sprinkling with Parmesan cheese.

3 Bake for 10 minutes to heat through. To finish, place under a hot griller to brown the topping.

GLYCAEMIC LOAD 1½

Per serve	
Energy	1910 kJ
Protein	29 g
Fat	9 g
Carbohydrate	61 g
Fibre	3 g
GI	Low

spiral pasta with smoked salmon, spinach and lemon sauce

serves 4 – 6

¾ cup vegetable stock
1 bunch English spinach, washed, stalks removed and shredded
juice and zest of ½ lemon
2 tablespoons low-fat ricotta cheese
300 g spiral pasta
200 g smoked salmon, chopped
cracked black pepper

1 Heat stock in a saucepan and add English spinach. Cover and cook for 2-3 minutes until wilted. Transfer to a food processor and purée. Add lemon juice and ricotta cheese, then stir in lemon zest.
2 Cook pasta in a large pot of boiling water and drain. Add spinach sauce and smoked salmon and toss. Season with cracked black pepper and serve immediately.

GLYCAEMIC LOAD 1½

Per serve	
Energy	1430 kJ
Protein	23 g
Fat	4 g
Carbohydrate	53 g
Fibre	5 g
GI	Low

glass noodle
and chicken salad

serves 4

3 tablespoons water

1 tablespoon fish sauce

2 tablespoons lemon juice

1 small chilli, de-seeded and finely chopped

1 tablespoon brown sugar

200 g lean chicken mince

100 g cellophane noodles (mung bean noodles),
   soaked in water for 10 minutes, then drained

2 green onions, roughly chopped

1 large red onion, thinly sliced

1 cups mixed fresh leaves of basil, coriander and mint

4 Chinese cabbage leaves

1 Heat water in a frypan and stir in fish sauce, lemon juice, chilli and brown sugar.

2 Add chicken and cook for a few minutes. Add noodles and more water, if necessary. Transfer to a bowl and mix in green onion, red onion and fresh herbs.

3 Place cabbage leaves in 4 deep noodle bowls and spoon over the chicken and noodle mixture. Serve immediately.

GLYCAEMIC LOAD 1

Per serve	
Energy	750 kJ
Protein	14 g
Fat	3 g
Carbohydrate	22 g
Fibre	2 g
GI	Low

char-grilled mustard chicken with peas and rissoni

serves 4

2 tablespoons Dijon mustard
1 tablespoon finely chopped chives
2 tablespoons buttermilk
500 g chicken tenderloins
16 wooden skewers, soaked in water for 30 minutes
150 g rissoni pasta
1 cup fresh or frozen peas, defrosted
¼ cup finely chopped parsley
2 tablespoons shredded fresh basil leaves
freshly ground pepper
2 tablespoons virgin olive oil

1 In a bowl, mix Dijon mustard, chives and buttermilk. Add chicken tenderloins and mix well. Marinate for 10 minutes. Thread onto wooden skewers and char-grill on preheated grill medium high for 5-6 minutes each side until cooked.

2 Bring a pot of water to the boil, add rissoni and cook for about 12 minutes until al dente. Drain and return to the saucepan.

3 In a separate saucepan, cook peas, drain and add to rissoni. Mix in parsley and basil leaves. Season with pepper and stir in oil. Spoon some rissoni onto each plate and top with char-grilled chicken skewers.

GLYCAEMIC LOAD ¾

Per serve	
Energy	1710 kJ
Protein	30 g
Fat	18 g
Carbohydrate	30 g
Fibre	4 g
GI	Low

spicy italian chicken with fussilli pasta

serves 4

2 tablespoons virgin olive oil

3 cloves garlic, crushed

1 large red onion, finely chopped

1 small red chilli, de-seeded and finely chopped

4 chicken Maryland (leg and thigh together), skin removed

300 ml light red wine

freshly ground black pepper

1 tablespoon drained chopped capers

1 tablespoon flat anchovies, drained and finely chopped

2 cups canned diced tomatoes

300 g fussilli pasta

freshly chopped parsley for garnish

1 Preheat oven to 180°C. In a large non-stick frypan, heat oil and cook garlic, onion and chilli over a low–medium heat until lightly browned and soft. Fry chicken in batches until lightly browned. Transfer to a casserole dish.

2 Add wine to frypan, season to taste with pepper and bring slowly to the boil. Simmer until half the liquid has evaporated. Pour over chicken and add capers, anchovies and tomatoes. Cover dish and bake in oven for about 30 minutes until chicken is tender.

3 Bring a large pot of salted water to the boil and cook pasta until al dente. To serve, spoon a little sauce over the pasta and top with chicken. Garnish with chopped fresh parsley.

GLYCAEMIC LOAD 1½

Per serve	
Energy	2520 kJ
Protein	39 g
Fat	20 g
Carbohydrate	57 g
Fibre	5 g
GI	Low

italian fennel and pasta soup

serves 4

1 tablespoon virgin olive oil

1 green capsicum, de-seeded and finely chopped

1 onion, finely chopped

1 medium bulb fennel, trimmed and finely chopped

3 cloves garlic, crushed

1 teaspoon crushed fennel seeds

5 cups chicken or vegetable stock

200 g fresh cheese ravioli or tortellini

3 zucchini, coarsely chopped

2 tablespoons light sour cream

2 tablespoons shredded fresh basil leaves

Parmesan cheese for grating

extra torn fresh basil leaves for garnish

1 In a large saucepan heat oil and add capsicum, onion, fennel, garlic and fennel seeds. Cook over a low heat, stirring occasionally, for 10-15 minutes until all vegetables are soft.

2 Pour in stock and bring to the boil. Simmer, covered, for 10 minutes. Stir in pasta and zucchini and cook for 8-10 minutes until pasta is cooked.

3 Stir in light sour cream and basil. Ladle into deep bowls and garnish with Parmesan cheese and extra basil leaves.

GLYCAEMIC LOAD ½

Per serve	
Energy	980 kJ
Protein	12 g
Fat	13 g
Carbohydrate	16 g
Fibre	4 g
GI	Low

green minestrone soup

serves 4

1 tablespoon virgin olive oil
2 sticks celery, finely chopped
1 large onion, finely chopped
2 leeks, washed and cut into thin slices
½ cup dry white wine
6 cups chicken stock
4 zucchini, trimmed and thinly sliced
¼ green cabbage, thinly shredded
½ cup farfalline, conchigliette piccole or stelline (tiny soup pasta)
freshly ground black pepper
1 bunch English spinach, washed, stems removed and shredded
½ cup fresh basil leaves
¼ cup freshly grated Parmesan cheese for garnish

1 In a saucepan, heat oil and cook celery, onion and leeks for 5 minutes, until soft. Add wine. Cover and cook for about 8 minutes until tender, stirring from time to time.
2 Add chicken stock and bring to the boil. Add zucchini, cabbage and pasta and cook for about 10 minutes, until pasta is tender.
3 Season to taste with pepper, stir in spinach and basil and cook for 2-3 minutes. Ladle into soup bowls and sprinkle with Parmesan cheese to serve.

GLYCAEMIC LOAD ¾

Per serve	
Energy	1100 kJ
Protein	12 g
Fat	8 g
Carbohydrate	23 g
Fibre	7 g
GI	Low

pasta, peas and herb frittata

serves 4

1 cup frozen peas, defrosted or fresh shelled
100 g fettuccini, cooked to al dente then roughly chopped
6 omega-enriched eggs, lightly beaten
½ cup fresh mint leaves, finely chopped
2 tablespoons finely chopped fresh dill
2 tablespoons fresh finely grated Parmesan cheese
ground black pepper
good pinch of ground nutmeg

1 Preheat oven to 180°C. Line a 20cm square baking tin with oven-bake paper. Mix all ingredients in a bowl. Spoon into tin and bake for about 30 minutes, until set.
2 Remove from oven and cool a little before turning out of the tin. Cut into squares and serve warm or cold with sliced tomatoes and salad leaves.

GLYCAEMIC LOAD ½

Per serve	
Energy	1000 kJ
Protein	16 g
Fat	9 g
Carbohydrate	21 g
Fibre	3 g
GI	Low

grilled fish with spinach pasta and mushrooms

serves 4

4 x 150 g fish fillets (ocean trout, Atlantic salmon, blue eye, swordfish steaks)
2 tablespoons virgin olive oil plus extra to brush fish
freshly ground pepper
200 g fresh spinach tagliatelli pasta
1 small onion, finely chopped
200 g mushrooms, wiped over and finely chopped
¼ cup finely chopped parsley
¼ cup finely chopped chives

1 Brush fish with a little oil and season with pepper. Cook pasta in a pot of boiling salted water for about 12 minutes, until al dente. Drain and return to the saucepan.
2 Heat oil in a frypan and cook onion for 3-4 minutes over a gentle heat. Stir in mushrooms and increase heat. Cook, stirring occasionally, for 6 minutes. Mix in pasta then stir in parsley and chives. Season with pepper.
3 Heat a char-grill pan to high and cook fish, skin side down, for 3-4 minutes. Reduce heat to medium, turn fish over and cook for a further 4-5 minutes until cooked through. To serve, spoon the pasta onto plates and top with grilled fish.

GLYCAEMIC LOAD 1

Per serve	
Energy	1900 kJ
Protein	37 g
Fat	16 g
Carbohydrate	37 g
Fibre	4 g
GI	Low

penne pasta salad with tuna and capsicum

serves 4

300 g dry penne pasta
1 tablespoon virgin olive oil
freshly ground black pepper
1 Spanish onion, thinly sliced
1 red capsicum, de-seeded and thinly sliced
1 green or yellow capsicum, de-seeded and thinly sliced
250 g yellow teardrop tomatoes, halved
1 cup stuffed green olives (with capsicum or feta), roughly chopped
1 x 225 g can tuna fillets, drained and flaked
1 tablespoon finely grated fresh Parmesan cheese
¼ cup chopped fresh parsley
¼ cup shredded basil leaves

Dressing
2 tablespoons virgin olive oil
2 tablespoons balsamic vinegar
2 cloves garlic, finely chopped

1 Cook pasta in a large pot of salted boiling water until al dente. Drain, toss with olive oil and season with pepper. Cool completely. Toss in remainder of salad ingredients.
2 Whisk together all dressing ingredients, add to salad and toss. Serve in pasta bowls.

GLYCAEMIC LOAD 1½

Per serve	
Energy	2010 kJ
Protein	17 g
Fat	19 g
Carbohydrate	56 g
Fibre	7 g
GI	Low

rissoni paella with pork

serves 4

1 tablespoon virgin olive oil
3 red onions, finely chopped
¼ cup hot salami, finely chopped
4 tablespoons fresh thyme leaves
3 large bay leaves
250 g lean pork, cut into bite-sized pieces
2 cups canned tomatoes, chopped and juice reserved
6 garlic cloves, finely chopped
1 good pinch of saffron threads, infused in ¼ cup water
freshly ground black pepper
300 g rissoni pasta, cooked
1 tablespoon finely chopped parsley

1 In a paella pan or large non-stick frypan, heat oil over a medium heat. Add onion, salami, fresh thyme leaves and bay leaves. Sauté until onion is soft and golden.
2 Add pork and cook for 3-4 minutes, until browned. Add tomatoes, garlic and saffron and season with pepper. Bring to the boil and cook at a simmer for 15-20 minutes until pork is tender and sauce has reduced.
3 Stir in cooked rissoni and season with pepper. Remove bay leaves and stir in chopped parsley. Serve immediately, garnished with lemon wedges and accompanied with chunks of fresh bread.

Winning tip
Rissoni pasta makes great pasta salads.
It can also be added to soups and casseroles.

GLYCAEMIC LOAD 2

Per serve	
Energy	2020 kJ
Protein	25 g
Fat	14 g
Carbohydrate	61 g
Fibre	6 g
GI	Low

rigatoni with sausages, mushrooms and zucchini

serves 4

1 tablespoon virgin olive oil

2 cloves garlic, finely sliced

1 red chilli, seeds removed and thinly sliced

4 chunky sausages (beef or pork), skins removed and sliced

250 g mushrooms, thinly sliced

2 large zucchini, peeled and thinly sliced

1 teaspoon dried oregano or 1 tablespoon fresh

400 g rigatoni pasta

4 tablespoons freshly grated Parmesan cheese

1 In a large non-stick frypan, heat oil and cook garlic and chilli over a low heat until golden.

2 Add sausage meat. Crumble with a wooden spoon to break meat into fine lumps. When brown, add mushrooms and zucchini and cook for 4-5 minutes until vegetables are soft. Stir in oregano.

3 Cook pasta in a large saucepan of boiling salted water until al dente. Drain and return pasta to the cooking pot. Add vegetable and sausage mixture and stir through. Serve in pasta bowls with a sprinkling of grated fresh Parmesan cheese.

GLYCAEMIC LOAD 2

Per serve	
Energy	2900 kJ
Protein	38 g
Fat	29 g
Carbohydrate	73 g
Fibre	9 g
GI	Low

japanese spicy beef and noodles

serves 4

250 g fillet of beef, very thinly sliced
2 tablespoons teriyaki sauce
5 cups chicken or beef stock
1 tablespoon chilli sauce
1 tablespoon fish sauce
1 tablespoon dry sherry
1 tablespoon sweet soy sauce
500 g fresh ramen noodles (wheat-based noodles)
4 red chillies, de-seeded and cut into thin strips
4 spring onions, finely chopped
4 sprigs mint
120 g bean sprouts
juice of 1 lime

1 Coat beef in teriyaki sauce and leave to marinate for at least 30 minutes. In a saucepan, heat stock with chilli sauce, fish sauce, dry sherry and sweet soy sauce and bring to the boil. Reduce heat to a simmer while you cook noodles and beef.

2 Cook noodles in boiling water for 2-3 minutes then drain. Spray a little oil into a non-stick frypan or wok and cook beef for 2-3 minutes over a high heat. Remove and put aside.

3 Place noodles into a deep bowl and ladle the soup over the noodles. Top with beef and garnish with sliced chillis, mint sprigs, spring onions and bean sprouts. Sprinkle with lime juice and serve immediately.

GLYCAEMIC LOAD 1

Per serve	
Energy	1110 kJ
Protein	21 g
Fat	5 g
Carbohydrate	31 g
Fibre	2 g
GI	Low

grains

The term 'grains' covers everything from bread through to cooked grains, such as couscous. Using different grains gives meals more variety, which is a vital part of food enjoyment. All grains soak up the liquid from a casserole or go with soup, and some grains are used to wrap food.

We have focused mainly on the highly convenient bread grain-type products. To achieve GI control, this bread is mainly wholegrain. Flat breads like mountain bread, pita and tortilla are also good.

The cooked grains we feature are moderate-GI alternatives to the classic rice, potatoes or pasta and are typically used as filling accompaniments. The most common of these grains are couscous, cornmeal, cracked wheat and barley.

Couscous is flour-coated semolina. It is usually sold as instant couscous, which means it has been pre-prepared and par-steamed.

Cornmeal, or polenta, is made from ground, dried corn kernels, either yellow or white. This versatile grain features widely in Italian cuisine. In northern Italy, polenta is cooked as a simple first course or as a side dish with a main meal or even as a hearty porridge. The porridge is made by cooking polenta with boiling water or milk until it is a sticky mass. About 300 g of polenta is cooked with about 1 litre of water. If served as a side dish, usually to accompany grilled meat dishes or roasts, it is typically flavoured with stock and herbs. Parmesan cheese, butter or marscapone may be stirred through at the end of the cooking; the dish is served soft. Another popular dish is made by spreading out cooked cooled polenta in a shallow tray, cutting it into squares or triangles then grilling or baking. It may be served with casseroles or topped with vegetables or grilled meats.

Cracked wheat is usually referred to as burghul or bulgar. It is made from wheat grains that have been hulled and steamed then cracked and dried. Especially good in salads and in pilafs, there are many recipes in which this versatile grain makes a great alternative to rice. Pour boiling water over it first and allow the liquid to be absorbed before using in salads.

Barley comes in many forms. Pearl barley can be cooked in a similar way to rice and is an unusual but flavoursome grain which goes well with rich meat or vegetarian dishes. Wholegrain barley, known as pot barley, takes longer to cook than pearl barley – it has not been polished like pearl barley. Barley flakes can be used in place of rolled oats and are often added to muesli.

contents

sweet potato cornbread

serves 4

1 cup polenta (cornmeal)
½ cup plain flour
2 teaspoons baking powder
2 tablespoons caster sugar or 2 tablespoons of Fruisana
1 large omega-enriched egg
2 tablespoons canola oil
1 cup low-fat buttermilk
1 large sweet potato (about 300 g), roasted and mashed
125 g can sweet corn kernels, drained and coarsely chopped
½ teaspoon chilli paste (optional)

1 Preheat oven to 190°C. Line a 20 cm square baking pan with oven-bake paper.
2 Mix all dry ingredients in a bowl. Whisk egg, oil, buttermilk, sweet potato, corn and chilli paste. Add to dry ingredients.
3 Pour batter into prepared tin and bake for 20-2 5 minutes, until cooked.

Winning tip
Serve sweet potato cornbread with casseroles as an alternative to rice or couscous. This bread is also delicious served with soup.

GLYCAEMIC LOAD 2¼   GLYCAEMIC LOAD 1½

WITH SUGAR   WITH FRUISANA

Per serve	
Energy	2500 kJ
Protein	13 g
Fat	15 g
Carbohydrate	64 g
Fibre	5 g
GI	Low

warm honey, pear and haloumi salad with roasted walnuts

serves 4

4 ripe pears
1 tablespoon honey
1 tablespoon sherry
1 tablespoon virgin olive oil
4 slices (100 g) Haloumi cheese
plain flour for dusting
1 cup wholegrain croutons
2 handfuls mixed salad leaves
50 g walnuts, toasted in the oven
1 Spanish onion, thinly sliced
freshly ground black pepper

Dressing
juice of 1 lemon
2 tablespoons virgin olive oil
freshly ground black pepper

1 Peel and core pears and cut into quarters. Mix honey and sherry in a bowl and brush over cut pears. Heat a non-stick frypan and add oil. Working in batches, cook pear pieces on each side until lightly browned. Remove to a bowl.
2 Cut Haloumi cheese into 8 slices, pat dry with kitchen paper and dust lightly with flour. In the non-stick frypan, working in batches, cook on either side until lightly browned.
3 Mix croutons through salad leaves, top with slices of pear and Haloumi cheese and scatter with walnuts and Spanish onion. Whisk together dressing ingredients and drizzle over salad. Season with black pepper. Serve warm.

Winning tip
This recipe highlights the problem of nutritionally important foods that don't appear to fit with our prescribed food guidelines. Although high in fat, cheese is a fantastic source of calcium, tastes great and is satisfying. In this recipe we keep the fat to appropriate levels by carefully selecting our oils and choosing a balance of ingredients. It's a mistake to live by numbers alone.

GLYCAEMIC LOAD 1¾

Per serve	
Energy	1800 kJ
Protein	10 g
Fat	27 g
Carbohydrate	43 g
Fibre	7 g
GI	Low

burghul, currants and pinenuts baked in red capsicums

serves 4

1 tablespoon virgin olive oil
1 medium onion, finely chopped
¼ teaspoon mixed spice
⅓ cup coarse burghul (cracked wheat)
¾ cup vegetable or chicken stock
⅓ cup dried currants
⅓ cup pinenuts, toasted
2 tablespoons chopped flat-leaf parsley
1 tablespoon grated lemon zest
4 red capsicums, tops removed and reserved, and de-seeded

1 Preheat oven to 180°C. Heat oil in a saucepan and cook onion and mixed spice over a low heat for 2-3 minutes. Stir in burghul, add stock and cook, stirring constantly.
2 Cover the pan and cook at a low simmer for 10 minutes. Remove and stir in the currants, pinenuts, parsley and lemon zest.
3 Spoon into capsicums and replace tops. Place in a lightly greased baking dish and cook for 30-40 minutes, until capsicums are tender. Serve immediately, accompanied with steamed green vegetables and a salad.

GLYCAEMIC LOAD 1

Per serve	
Energy	990 kJ
Protein	7 g
Fat	9 g
Carbohydrate	28 g
Fibre	6 g
GI	Low

stuffed gratin capsicums

serves 4

4 large yellow or red capsicums

2 tablespoons olive oil

1 medium firm eggplant, chopped

2 cloves garlic, finely chopped

1 cup mashed chickpeas

1 x 425 g can chopped tomatoes

4 tablespoons finely chopped parsley

4 slices wholegrain bread, blended to breadcrumbs

50 g freshly grated Parmesan cheese

3 grates of nutmeg

ground black pepper to taste

2 cups vegetable stock

1 Preheat oven to 180°C. Slice capsicums in half lengthways to make 8 'cups'. Remove seeds and pith and blanch for 5 minutes in boiling water to soften. Drain, then place in a baking dish.

2 Heat oil in a frypan and lightly fry chopped eggplant and garlic until soft. Remove from heat and stir in chickpeas, tomatoes and parsley. Spoon mixture into capsicum halves.

3 Mix breadcrumbs, Parmesan cheese, nutmeg and pepper and sprinkle over eggplant filling. Pour vegetable stock into baking dish and cover with foil.

4 Bake for about 40-50 minutes, then remove foil for 5 minutes to allow topping to crisp up. Serve hot or cold with salad.

GLYCAEMIC LOAD ¾

Per serve	
Energy	1940 kJ
Protein	15 g
Fat	15 g
Carbohydrate	32 g
Fibre	8 g
GI	Low

eggplant rolls stuffed with couscous, green beans and mint

serves 4

3 tablespoons olive oil

1 large red onion

200 g green beans

140 g couscous, prepared according to packet instructions

2 tablespoons raisins, soaked

6 carrots, peeled and finely grated

1 cup fresh mint, finely chopped

3 tablespoons Greek yoghurt

3 large eggplants, sliced thinly lengthways

1 In a frypan, heat oil and cook onion until soft. Add beans and cook until tender. In a bowl, mix couscous, raisins, carrots, mint and yoghurt then stir in the onion and green beans.

2 Grill eggplant slices until soft and browned. Remove from griller and cool slightly. Place a tablespoon of couscous mixture onto each slice of eggplant and roll up. Serve at room temperature.

Winning tip
Couscous is wonderfully simple to prepare, but if you have leftover burghul pilaf to hand, try this as the eggplant stuffing for an interesting change of direction.

GLYCAEMIC LOAD ¾

Per serve	
Energy	1120 kJ
Protein	7 g
Fat	14 g
Carbohydrate	24 g
Fibre	8 g
GI	Low

mushrooms roasted with pinenuts on grilled sour dough with goat's curd cheese

serves 4

16 large flat field mushrooms
juice of ½ lemon
2 tablespoons virgin olive oil
2 cloves garlic, peeled and crushed
⅓ cup soft wholegrain breadcrumbs
¼ teaspoons chopped fresh thyme leaves
freshly ground black pepper
⅓ cup roasted pinenuts
4 slices sourdough bread, grilled
25 g soft goat's curd cheese

1 Preheat oven to 200°C. Line a baking tray with oven-bake paper. Wipe mushrooms with a damp cloth. Remove stems, chop finely and put aside. Dip mushroom caps into lemon juice then arrange in baking dish, stem side up.

2 In a non-stick frypan, heat oil and sauté breadcrumbs, thyme and chopped mushroom caps for 2-3 minutes. Season well with pepper then stir in pinenuts. Remove from heat.

3 Spoon mixture into mushroom caps and bake for 15-20 minutes. Place on a bed of mixed leaf salad and serve with grilled sourdough bread smeared with a little goat's curd cheese on the side.

GLYCAEMIC LOAD 1

Per serve	
Energy	1500 kJ
Protein	12 g
Fat	20 g
Carbohydrate	27 g
Fibre	6 g
GI	Low

mushroom and pearl barley soup

serves 4

2 tablespoons virgin olive oil
1 onion, finely chopped
2 cloves garlic, finely chopped
2 large sticks celery, finely chopped
500 g mushrooms, wiped clean and roughly chopped
¼ cup pearl barley
5 cups chicken stock
1 potato, peeled and roughly grated
¼ cup finely chopped fresh parsley
freshly ground pepper
Italian parsley leaves, chopped, for garnish

1 Heat oil in a saucepan and add onion, garlic, celery, mushrooms and barley. Cook over a low heat for 20 minutes, until mushrooms are soft.
2 Pour in stock and grated potato and bring to the boil. Cover and simmer for 40 minutes until barley is tender and soup has thickened.
3 Stir in parsley and season with pepper. To serve, ladle into bowls and garnish with Italian parsley.

GLYCAEMIC LOAD ½

Per serve	
Energy	960 kJ
Protein	10 g
Fat	11 g
Carbohydrate	18 g
Fibre	6 g
GI	Low

fresh tomato and bread soup

serves 4

2 tablespoons virgin olive oil

1 onion, chopped

1 fresh small red chilli (optional), de-seeded and chopped

4 cloves garlic, chopped

½ cup dry white wine

1 kg ripe tomatoes, skinned, de-seeded and chopped, or 2 x 425 g cans

good pinch of white sugar

ground black pepper

1 cup chicken stock

150 g day-old sourdough bread, crust removed

1 cup firmly packed torn basil leaves

1 tablespoon extra virgin olive oil to drizzle for garnish

torn basil leaves for garnish

1 Heat olive oil in a large saucepan and cook onion over a low heat until soft. Add chilli, garlic and wine and cook over a high heat until reduced.

2 Add tomatoes, season with sugar and black pepper to taste, bring to the boil and cook over a medium heat, stirring occasionally, for about 30 minutes until tomato is thick and concentrated. Pour in about 300 ml stock and cook for a further 5 minutes.

3 Cut bread into large pieces and add to soup. Stir over a low heat until bread absorbs liquid (add a little more stock if soup is too thick).

4 Remove from heat, stir in basil leaves and adjust seasoning, if necessary. Stand for 5 minutes. To serve, ladle soup into warm serving bowls. Drizzle with olive oil and garnish with torn basil leaves.

Winning tip
To peel tomatoes, cut a cross at the stalk end, plunge tomatoes into boiling water for 2-3 minutes then remove. Cool a little before peeling off the skin.
Cut in half and remove the seeds with a teaspoon.
If kitchen preparation time is short, use 2 x 425 g cans of diced tomatoes.

GLYCAEMIC LOAD 1

Per serve	
Energy	1500 kJ
Protein	10 g
Fat	16 g
Carbohydrate	27 g
Fibre	7 g
GI	Low

hearty minestrone with parmesan dumplings

serves 4 – 6

1 tablespoon virgin olive oil

1 onion, peeled and roughly chopped

3 carrots, peeled and cut into small chunks

1 fennel bulb, trimmed and roughly chopped

1 small red capsicum, de-seeded and cut into strips

100 g French beans, topped and tailed and cut into small chunks

¼ green cabbage, finely shredded

4 cups beef stock

1 glass red wine (120 ml)

1 x 425 g can chopped tomatoes

2 teaspoons dried oregano

2 Italian sausages, cut into small pieces

2 tablespoons roughly chopped fresh spinach leaves

shaved Parmesan cheese for garnish

Parmesan Dumplings

2 slices wholegrain bread, crusts removed

3 tablespoons freshly grated Parmesan cheese

good pinch of dry mustard powder

freshly ground black pepper

1 small omega-enriched egg, lightly beaten

GLYCAEMIC LOAD ¾

Per serve	
Energy	1600 kJ
Protein	26 g
Fat	20 g
Carbohydrate	28 g
Fibre	11 g
GI	Low

1 Begin with Parmesan Dumplings. In a food processor, blend bread into fine breadcrumbs. Stir in Parmesan cheese, mustard powder and pepper. Stir in enough beaten egg to bind mixture. Form into small balls and chill until ready to cook.

2 In a saucepan, heat oil, add onion and cook over a low heat until soft. Add carrots, fennel, red capsicum, green beans and cook, stirring, for 3-4 minutes. Stir in cabbage and cook for 5 minutes, stirring occasionally.

3 Add stock, red wine, tomatoes and oregano. Slowly bring to the boil and cook at a simmer for 20-30 minutes until vegetables are just tender.

4 Stir in sausage and spinach. Cook for 3-4 minutes then drop in the Parmesan Dumplings. Cook for 1-2 minutes, until dumplings are firm. Season with pepper. To serve, ladle into bowls and garnish with shaved Parmesan cheese.

Winning tip
These easy-to-make dumplings are an interesting way of adding flavour to a classic Italian soup. Alternatively, omit the sausage and the dumplings and substitute meat tortellini.

grilled pork chops with fennel and chive burghul pilaf

serves 4

1 tablespoon olive oil
1 red onion, finely chopped
1 bulb of fennel, finely chopped
150 g burghul (cracked wheat)
4 spring onions, finely chopped
3 tablespoons finely chopped garlic chives
1⅓ cups chicken or vegetable stock
ground black pepper
1 tablespoon chopped toasted macadamia nuts
4 pork chops, trimmed of fat and seasoned with ground black pepper

1 In a saucepan, heat oil and cook onion and fennel over a medium heat until soft. Add burghul and cook for 1-2 minutes. Stir in spring onions and garlic chives and cook for 2-3 minutes.
2 Pour in stock and bring to the boil. Cover and cook over a low heat for 30 minutes until burghul is tender. Season well with pepper and stir in macadamia nuts.
3 Preheat grill pan or barbecue grill. Cook chops for 4-5 minutes each side, depending on thickness. Serve with burghul pilaf and salad.

Winning tip
If fennel is not in season, use 3 sticks of celery instead.

GLYCAEMIC LOAD ¾

Per serve	
Energy	1640 kJ
Protein	35 g
Fat	13 g
Carbohydrate	28 g
Fibre	4 g
GI	Low

italian pork and veal meatballs

serves 4

500 g pork and veal mince
1 cup wholegrain breadcrumbs
1 teaspoon grated fresh lemon zest
1 omega-enriched egg
¼ cup chopped fresh flat-leaf parsley
1 tablespoon freshly grated Parmesan cheese
1 tablespoon olive oil
1 large onion, finely chopped
1 x 425 g can diced tomatoes
1 cup beef or vegetable stock
2 tablespoons stuffed green olives, roughly chopped
freshly ground black pepper
2 tablespoons flat-leaf parsley for garnish

1 Mix mince, breadcrumbs, lemon zest, egg, parsley and Parmesan cheese until well combined. Form into 12 even sized meatballs and put aside.
2 Heat oil in a saucepan and cook onion over a medium heat until soft. Stir in tomatoes, vegetable stock and olives. Bring to the boil and reduce to a simmer.
3 Gently lower meatballs into liquid and cover the pan. Cook over a gentle heat for 30-40 minutes until meatballs are cooked. Season with pepper and garnish with flat-leaf parsley. Serve with spaghetti or rice with grated fresh Parmesan on the side to make up required carbohydrate.

GLYCAEMIC LOAD ½

Per serve	
Energy	1510 kJ
Protein	36 g
Fat	12 g
Carbohydrate	24 g
Fibre	5 g
GI	Low

beef and spinach rolls

serves 4

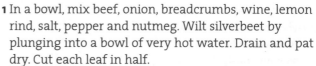

400 g lean minced beef

1 onion, grated

2 slices wholegrain bread, made into breadcrumbs

1 tablespoon red wine or beef stock

2 teaspoons grated lemon rind

pinch of salt

½ teaspoon freshly ground black pepper

pinch of ground nutmeg

6 silverbeet leaves, stalks removed

1 x 425 g can chopped tomatoes

juice of 1 lemon

freshly ground black pepper

2 tablespoons chopped fresh parsley

1 In a bowl, mix beef, onion, breadcrumbs, wine, lemon rind, salt, pepper and nutmeg. Wilt silverbeet by plunging into a bowl of very hot water. Drain and pat dry. Cut each leaf in half.

2 Place a piece of spinach on a flat surface. Take a meatball-sized quantity of mince and wrap up carefully in spinach to form a neat package. You should have sufficient to make approximately 12 spinach rolls.

3 Place tomatoes and lemon juice in a large saucepan and season with pepper to taste. Place spinach rolls in liquid. Cover and gently bring to the boil. Simmer for 35-40 minutes until cooked through. Serve immediately, spooning onto shallow bowls of pasta or boiled Doongara rice – enough to make the meal up to the carbohydrate level you desire – and garnish with chopped parsley.

GLYCAEMIC LOAD ½

Per serve	
Energy	1840 kJ
Protein	24 g
Fat	7 g
Carbohydrate	15 g
Fibre	3 g
GI	Low

couscous salad in pocket bread with grilled steak

serves 4

1½ cups rehydrated couscous (pour hot water over ¾ cups
    couscous, cover and leave to stand for 3-4 minutes)
½ cup diced cucumber
2 spring onions, finely chopped
2 tablespoons freshly chopped mint
1 tomato, roughly chopped
juice of ½ lemon
2 tablespoons olive oil
ground black pepper
2 trim rump steaks (about 200 g each)
4 small wholemeal pocket breads

1 In a large bowl, combine couscous, cucumber, spring
  onions, mint, tomato, lemon juice and olive oil.
  Season with ground black pepper.
2 Preheat char-grill and cook steak for 4-5 minutes each
  side. Rest for 5 minutes before carving into thin strips.
3 Spoon a little salad and steak into each pocket bread.
  Serve immediately with a little tomato sauce on the side.

GLYCAEMIC LOAD 1

Per serve	
Energy	1210 kJ
Protein	16 g
Fat	12 g
Carbohydrate	29 g
Fibre	3 g
GI	Low

chicken caesar salad

serves 4

1 cup chicken stock
2 chicken breast fillets
2 mixed-grain muffins
1 tablespoon virgin olive oil
1 clove garlic
4 thin slices prosciutto
1 omega-enriched egg
½ cos lettuce, washed and torn into pieces
2 tablespoons freshly grated Parmesan cheese

Dressing
2 tablespoons virgin olive oil
1 teaspoon Dijon mustard
2 tablespoons lemon juice
generous grinding of black pepper

1 Preheat oven to 200°C. Heat stock in a saucepan, add chicken fillets and cover. Poach over a gentle heat for about 10 minutes. Turn off heat and cool in the stock for a further 10 minutes. Remove from pan and slice into thin pieces.

2 Rub muffins with oil and garlic. Bake for 5-8 minutes, until toasted and browned. Remove from oven and cut into small chunks. Place prosciutto on a baking tray and grill or bake until crisp.

3 Bring a small pan of water to the boil and cook egg for about 1 minute. Remove and cool under running water.

4 In a large salad bowl, place chicken, lettuce, garlic croutons and Parmesan cheese. Crumble in prosciutto. Break egg into salad and stir through the leaves. Finally, whisk together all dressing ingredients. Pour over salad, toss and serve immediately.

> **Winning tip**
> *Variations abound on the ever-popular Caesar Salad. If you prefer yours prepared the classic way, with anchovies, add a few with the Parmesan cheese and omit the prosciutto.*

GLYCAEMIC LOAD ½

Per serve	
Energy	2070 kJ
Protein	43 g
Fat	30 g
Carbohydrate	13 g
Fibre	2 g
GI	Low

chicken skewers with pearl barley and lemon risotto

serves 4

2 chicken breast fillets, each cut into 6 thin strips

12 bamboo skewers, soaked in water for 30 minutes

1 tablespoon virgin olive oil

1 teaspoon lemon thyme leaves

1 clove garlic, crushed

100 g pearl barley

1 small onion, peeled and finely chopped

2 bay leaves

2 litres chicken stock

finely grated zest and juice of 1 lemon

¼ cup finely chopped parsley

salt

freshly ground black pepper

1 Toss chicken in oil, lemon thyme and garlic. Thread onto skewers and put aside until ready to cook.

2 Place pearl barley, onion and bay leaves in a heavy-based saucepan. Place over a medium heat, slowly add about ¼ cup of stock and bring to the boil. Add another ¼ cup stock and keep stirring until stock has been absorbed. Continue in this way until all stock has been used.

3 Stir in lemon zest, lemon juice and parsley and season with salt and pepper.

4 Preheat a char-grill plate and cook chicken for 4-5 minutes each side until lightly browned. Serve immediately over barley risotto.

GLYCAEMIC LOAD ½

Per serve	
Energy	1570 kJ
Protein	40 g
Fat	15 g
Carbohydrate	18 g
Fibre	3 g
GI	Low

couscous with chorizo and chicken

serves 4

1 tablespoon olive oil
1 clove garlic, finely chopped
4 chicken thigh fillets, sliced into 8 pieces
1 chorizo sausage, skin removed and cut into thin slices
1 x 425 g can diced tomatoes
½ teaspoon of ground sweet paprika
½ teaspoon freshly ground black pepper
1¼ cups frozen peas, defrosted
1 cup chicken stock
1 cup couscous
6 semi-sun-dried tomatoes
3 tablespoons Italian parsley, chopped

1 Heat oil in a non-stick frypan and cook garlic over a medium heat for 1 minute. Working in batches, stir in chicken and cook for 4-5 minutes, until browned. Remove from heat and put aside.

2 Add chorizo to frypan and cook for 1-2 minutes. Return chicken to the pan and stir in tomatoes, sweet paprika, black pepper and peas. Bring to the boil and simmer for 6-8 minutes, until chicken and peas are cooked.

3 Heat stock in a saucepan until boiling. Stir in couscous and semi-sun-dried tomatoes. Cover and remove from heat. Rest for 5 minutes, then stir into the frypan with chicken and chorizo. Mix through and stir in the parsley. Serve immediately, accompanied with mixed leaf salad.

GLYCAEMIC LOAD 1½

Per serve	
Energy	1940 kJ
Protein	32 g
Fat	22 g
Carbohydrate	32 g
Fibre	5 g
GI	Low

tortilla chicken bake

serves 4

1 large chicken breast fillet cut Into small pieces (250-300 g)

¼ cup polenta (cornmeal)

2 tablespoons light olive oil

1 small onion, finely chopped

2 cloves garlic, finely chopped

4 zucchini, cut into small chunks

1 cup canned tomatoes plus extra ½ cup

½ cup chicken stock

½ cup corn kernels

3 x 20 cm soft tortillas

¼ cup tasty cheese, grated

1 Preheat oven to 180°C. Place chicken in a mixing bowl. Add polenta and stir to coat chicken. Heat oil in a large saucepan. Add chicken and fry for 2 – 3 minutes, until lightly browned. Remove to a plate.

2 Add onion and garlic to frypan and cook for 2 – 3 minutes until softened. Add zucchini and 1 cup of the tomatoes. Return chicken to saucepan. Bring to the boil and simmer for 10 minutes.

3 Spray a 20 cm round baking dish with oil. Cover base with a tortilla and spoon on half the chicken mixture. Top with second tortilla. Spoon on remainder of chicken and top with the third tortilla. Spread on the remaining ½ cup tomatoes and sprinkle with cheese.

4 Bake for 25 – 30 minutes until cheese has melted and top browned. Remove from oven and cool a little before serving.

Winning tip
Essentially, this is a Mexican-style chicken lasagne. If you don't have a round baking dish, cut the tortilla to fit a square or rectangular oven-to-table dish.

GLYCAEMIC LOAD 1¼

Per serve	
Energy	1620 kJ
Protein	24 g
Fat	17 g
Carbohydrate	30 g
Fibre	6 g
GI	Low

sesame oat chicken

serves 4

1 cup rolled oats
1 teaspoon dried tarragon
ground black pepper
2 tablespoons sesame seeds
500 g chicken breast fillets, cut into thick wedges
¼ cup buttermilk
2 tablespoons olive oil
lemon wedges for garnish

1 Preheat oven to 200°C. In a food processor, blend rolled oats until finely ground. Combine with dried tarragon, pepper and sesame seeds and place on a flat plate.
2 Dip chicken pieces in buttermilk then roll in oat mixture and put aside. In a non-stick frypan, heat oil and brown each chicken piece on both sides.
3 Transfer to baking tray lined with oven-bake paper. Bake for 15 – 20 minutes, until chicken is cooked through. To serve, garnish with lemon wedges and accompany with steamed green vegetables or mixed leaf salad.

Winning tip
This simple but effective coating is also delicious on fish fillets, pork or veal schnitzel.

GLYCAEMIC LOAD ½

Per serve	
Energy	1570 kJ
Protein	31 g
Fat	20 g
Carbohydrate	15 g
Fibre	2 g
GI	Low

warm pita bread salad with feta and olives

serves 4

2 Spanish onions, each cut into 8 wedges

2 red capsicums, de-seeded and cut into chunks

1 tablespoon virgin olive oil

2 teaspoons balsamic vinegar

1 teaspoon sugar

4 small wholemeal pita pocket breads

200 g baby spinach leaves

4 green onions, roughly chopped

1 cup flat-leaf parsley leaves

¼ cup roughly chopped Kalamata olives

⅓ cup feta cheese, crumbled

Dressing

1 tablespoon chopped mint leaves

2 teaspoons toasted sesame seeds

2 teaspoons grated zest

2 tablespoons fresh lemon juice

2 tablespoons virgin olive oil

1 Preheat oven to 200°C. Whisk together dressing ingredients and put aside. Place onion and capsicum on an oven tray, drizzle with olive oil and balsamic vinegar then sprinkle with sugar and bake for 20 minutes.

2 Place pita bread on an oven tray and bake for about 10 minutes until crisp, or grill on both sides until crisp.

3 Break toasted pita bread into small pieces and mix with roasted onion and capsicum. Add spinach, green onions and parsley and combine.

4 Pour dressing over salad and toss. Top with olives and feta cheese and serve immediately.

GLYCAEMIC LOAD 1¼

Per serve	
Energy	1520 kJ
Protein	13 g
Fat	18 g
Carbohydrate	33 g
Fibre	7 g
GI	Low

lamb korma with mango chutney on turkish bread

serves 4

½ cup korma paste

⅓ cup plain low-fat yoghurt plus extra ¼ cup for garnish

1 tablespoon lemon or lime juice

400 g lamb filets

½ regular-sized loaf of Turkish bread, split lengthwise, brushed with oil and grilled

¼ cup mango chutney

100 g mixed baby salad leaves

½ cup fresh mint leaves

1 Preheat oven to 220°C. Combine korma paste and ⅓ cup of the yoghurt. Smear over lamb and marinate for 20 minutes.

2 Place lamb on baking tray and cook for 20 minutes. Remove from oven, cover lightly with foil and rest for 10 minutes. Slice into thin strips.

3 Cut grilled Turkish bread into 4 squares and spread with a little mango chutney. Top with mixed leaves and lamb slices, and finish off with a dollop of yoghurt and mint leaves. Serve immediately.

Winning tip
For a more authentic Indian-style dish, serve with dosai or Tandoori bread that has been grilled or baked until crisp.

GLYCAEMIC LOAD 1½

Per serve	
Energy	1210 kJ
Protein	22 g
Fat	11 g
Carbohydrate	22 g
Fibre	4 g
GI	Medium

legumes

The name legume covers many plants with seedpods that split open when ripe. The pods may contain peas, beans or lentils. Peanuts, carob and tamarind are also classed as legumes. Dried seeds are called pulses.

Although legumes make up one of the most useful low-GI ingredient groups, many of us find them intimidating. To break down that barrier, think 'canned'. The wide range of canned products you can buy is just as nutritious and as low-GI as the legumes prepared in the home kitchen. The texture of the canned varieties is slightly different and, of course, when cooking dried pulses you can add flavours like onion, garlic, herbs and stock. In terms of quantity, 100 g of dried beans are equivalent to 400 g of canned beans.

Not too many years ago, dried products were vital to many communities as this was their major or back-up protein food for the entire year. That is why many traditional recipes suggest using dried legumes. Simply skip ahead and substitute our modern canned products, and the recipes will still work.

Using dried legumes

Store your dried produce in airtight containers. Here is a guide to soaking and cooking times:

	soak	cook
Lima beans	overnight	30 minutes
Butterbeans	overnight	2 hours
Pinto beans	overnight	1½ – 2 hours
Black beans	overnight	1 hour
Black-eyed beans	overnight	45 minutes
Soybeans	overnight	2 – 2½ hours
Broad beans	overnight	1½ hours
Flageolets	overnight	45 minutes
Chickpeas	overnight	2 – 3 hours
Split peas	30 minutes	1½ – 2 hours
Red kidney beans	3 hours	20 minutes
Lentils, split lentils	no soaking time	20 – 30 minutes

Dry beans double in bulk after cooking, e.g. 50 g dried lentils will be enough for about 4 serves when cooked.

Before cooking, wash the dried pulses under cold running water. Drain and pick out any stones or grit. Pre-soak in a large bowl or pan with plenty of water for the required time. Drain well and place in a large saucepan and cover with plenty of water.

Bring to the boil and cook at a rapid boil for at least 10 minutes. Skim off any scum during the cooking time. Cook with a pan lid on and do not add any salt, as this will toughen the skins. Stir in 1 – 2 teaspoons of olive oil during the cooking to prevent the pulses from boiling over and to give them a creamy texture. Season after they are cooked and drained.

contents

pea and ham soup

serves 4

2 tablespoons olive oil

1 large onion, peeled and finely chopped

2 cloves garlic, finely chopped

100 g speck ham, finely chopped

1 bay leaf

½ cup yellow split peas, washed and picked over

½ cup green split peas, washed and picked over

6 cups water

pinch of salt

¼ teaspoon ground black pepper

½ cup finely chopped parsley

½ cup toasted wholegrain croutons

1 In a saucepan, heat oil and cook onion and garlic over a low heat until soft. Stir in ham and cook for 2 – 3 minutes.

2 Add bay leaf, split peas, water, salt and pepper. Bring to the boil and cover. Simmer for 45 minutes to 1 hour until split peas are cooked and soup has thickened.

3 Remove bay leaf and stir in chopped parsley. Ladle into soup bowls and garnish with wholegrain croutons.

GLYCAEMIC LOAD ¾

Per serve	
Energy	1450 kJ
Protein	20 g
Fat	12 g
Carbohydrate	36 g
Fibre	8 g
GI	Low

rustic white bean and leek soup

serves 4

2 tablespoons virgin olive oil
2 large leeks, washed and thinly sliced
4 garlic cloves, finely chopped
¼ teaspoon dried tarragon
2 cups chicken stock
2 cans white beans, rinsed (about 2 cups)
1 cup milk
pinch of salt
freshly ground black pepper
2 tablespoons fresh lemon juice
2 tablespoons finely chopped parsley for garnish

1 In a saucepan, heat oil and add leeks, garlic and tarragon. Cook for 4 – 5 minutes over a medium heat until soft. Pour in stock and bring to the boil. Simmer for 5 – 6 minutes.
2 Place white beans and 1 cup of the hot stock in a food processor then purée. Return to the pan and stir in milk. Gently re-heat then cook for 3 – 4 minutes.
3 Season to taste and stir in lemon juice. Ladle into soup bowls and garnish with parsley.

GLYCAEMIC LOAD ¼

Per serve	
Energy	890 kJ
Protein	11 g
Fat	10 g
Carbohydrate	17 g
Fibre	7 g
GI	Low

lamb kofta with spicy red lentil broth

serves 4-6

500 g lean minced lamb
1 small onion, finely chopped
2 cloves garlic, crushed
1 omega-enriched egg, lightly beaten
2 tablespoons virgin olive oil
1 onion, finely chopped
4 tomatoes, peeled, de-seeded and roughly chopped,
   or 1 x 425 g can tomatoes
1 teaspoon ground cumin
1 teaspoon ground turmeric
1 teaspoon ground coriander
¼ teaspoon ground cinnamon
1 teaspoon chilli paste
4 cups vegetable stock
150 g red lentils
juice of 1 lime
4 tablespoons plain low-fat yoghurt
½ cup coriander leaves for garnish

1 Mix lamb mince, onion, garlic and egg. Shape mixture into walnut-sized balls and refrigerate until ready to cook.
2 In a saucepan, heat oil and add onion, tomatoes, spices and chilli paste. Cook over a gentle heat until tomatoes are soft and syrupy.
3 Add stock and lentils and bring to the boil. Simmer, covered, for 20 minutes then add the lamb kofta. Return to the boil and simmer for 15 – 20 minutes, until lentils and kofta are cooked.
4 Stir in lime juice and adjust seasoning if necessary. Ladle into deep bowls and garnish with a dollop of yoghurt and coriander leaves.

GLYCAEMIC LOAD ½

Per serve	
Energy	1930 kJ
Protein	44 g
Fat	17 g
Carbohydrate	27 g
Fibre	9 g
GI	Low

butternut pumpkin stuffed with spicy borlotti beans

serves 4

1 tablespoon virgin olive oil

1 medium onion, finely chopped

1 garlic clove, finely chopped

2 teaspoons ground cumin

1 teaspoon ground coriander

pinch of cayenne pepper

2 tomatoes, de-seeded and roughly chopped

1 cup canned Borlotti beans, drained and rinsed

2 tablespoons chopped flat-leaf parsley

1 tablespoon grated lemon zest

½ cup wholegrain breadcrumbs, toasted

1 butternut pumpkin, halved, de-seeded and blanched in boiling water for 5 minutes

1 Preheat oven to 180°C. Heat oil in a saucepan and add onion and garlic. Cook over a low heat for 2 – 3 minutes.

2 Add spices and tomatoes and cook for 3 – 4 minutes. Stir in Borlotti beans and cook for 5 minutes. Remove from heat and stir in parsley, lemon zest and breadcrumbs.

3 Spoon into pumpkin halves, piling mixture high. Place in a lightly greased baking dish, cover with foil and cook for 30 – 35 minutes, until pumpkin is tender. Serve immediately with steamed green vegetables or a salad.

GLYCAEMIC LOAD 1½

Per serve	
Energy	1190 kJ
Protein	12 g
Fat	6 g
Carbohydrate	44 g
Fibre	7 g
GI	Low

char-grilled vegetable and bean gratin with fresh basil

serves 4

1 large eggplant, peeled and sliced thinly lengthways
3 medium zucchini, sliced thinly lengthways
1 tablespoon olive oil
1 medium red onion, finely chopped
2 cloves garlic, finely chopped
1 x 400 g can cannellini beans, drained and rinsed
1 x 425 g can diced tomatoes
freshly ground black pepper
1 cup fresh wholegrain breadcrumbs
2 tablespoons Parmesan cheese, finely grated
1 cup fresh basil leaves

1 Preheat oven to 180°C. Heat a char-grill pan and cook eggplant and zucchini on both sides until lightly charred and softened.
2 Heat oil in a non-stick frypan and cook onions and garlic over a gentle heat until soft. Remove from heat and stir in cannellini beans.
3 Line sides and bottom of a gratin dish with eggplant and zucchini, spoon over half the bean mixture, then half the tomatoes, seasoning each layer with pepper. Repeat, finishing with a layer of tomatoes.
4 In a food processor, blend breadcrumbs, Parmesan and basil leaves until well combined. Sprinkle over gratin, then bake for 30 – 40 minutes, until lightly browned. Serve hot with a mixed-leaf salad.

> **Winning tip**
> *Depending what vegetables are in season, try char-grilling red or yellow capsicums and thin slices of fennel instead of eggplant and zucchini.*

GLYCAEMIC LOAD ¾

Per serve	
Energy	1340 kJ
Protein	17 g
Fat	8 g
Carbohydrate	40 g
Fibre	14 g
GI	Low

grilled field mushrooms with lentil and walnut pâté

serves 4-6

1 x 400 g can lentils, drained
1 teaspoon ground turmeric
4 cloves garlic, crushed
pinch of salt
5 tablespoons lemon juice
1 cup vegetable stock
1 tablespoon sweet soy sauce
½ cup walnuts, lightly toasted in the oven for 4–5 minutes
4 flat field mushrooms
1 tablespoon virgin olive oil
freshly ground black pepper
salad leaves

1 In a saucepan, heat lentils, turmeric, garlic, salt, lemon juice and stock. Bring to the boil and simmer, uncovered, for about 8 minutes. Remove from heat and cool a little.
2 Transfer to a food processor, add sweet soy sauce and toasted walnuts and blend.
3 Brush field mushrooms with a little olive oil and season with pepper. Heat a char-grill pan over a high heat and grill mushrooms for 3 – 4 minutes each side until wilted and soft. Arrange on plates over salad leaves and serve with a spoonful of lentil pâté.

Winning tip
Try this lentil pâté on toasted wholegrain bread with pan-fried thinly sliced button mushrooms or grilled prosciutto over the top.

GLYCAEMIC LOAD ½

Per serve	
Energy	1100 kJ
Protein	12 g
Fat	16 g
Carbohydrate	19 g
Fibre	7 g
GI	Low

fine lentil salad with capsicums, red onions and feta

serves 4

1 cup fine green lentils
4 whole cloves garlic
3 bay leaves
pinch of oregano

Salad
1 red capsicum, finely chopped
1 red onion, finely chopped
18 Kalamata olives, stones removed
150 g Greek feta, gently crumbled
3 tablespoons finely chopped fresh mint
1 bunch rocket

Dressing
3 tablespoons extra virgin olive oil
1½ tablespoons red wine vinegar
pinch of ground cumin
salt
freshly ground black pepper

1 Place lentils in a saucepan with garlic, bay leaves and oregano. Cover with water to about 5 cm above the lentils. Bring to the boil and simmer for 30 minutes, uncovered, until tender. Remove from heat, drain and cool.

2 Whisk all dressing ingredients in a bowl and pour over the lentils. Add capsicum and onion and toss. When ready to serve, sprinkle with olives, feta and chopped mint. Serve on a bed of rocket leaves.

GLYCAEMIC LOAD ½

Per serve	
Energy	1650 kJ
Protein	23 g
Fat	21 g
Carbohydrate	25 g
Fibre	10 g
GI	Low

lentil and vegetable moussaka

serves 4

1 medium eggplant, cut into rounds
4 small potatoes, sliced, about 200 g
olive oil spray
1 large onion, finely chopped
1 red capsicum, finely chopped
1 large clove garlic, finely chopped
5 tablespoons red wine or vegetable stock
2 tablespoons tomato purée
½ teaspoon ground allspice
¼ teaspoon ground cinnamon
1 x 410 g can brown lentils, drained
salt
freshly ground black pepper

Topping
3 omega-enriched eggs
6 tablespoons plain low-fat yoghurt
3 tablespoons Parmesan cheese, grated
freshly ground nutmeg

GLYCAEMIC LOAD 1

Per serve	
Energy	1050 kJ
Protein	16 g
Fat	7 g
Carbohydrate	25 g
Fibre	6 g
GI	Low

1 Preheat oven to 180°C. Preheat a char-grill pan and grill eggplant slices for 2 – 3 minutes each side. Char-grill potato slices for 3 – 4 minutes each side, spraying with olive oil as required during cooking. Remove from heat and put aside.

2 Heat oil in a non-stick frypan and cook onion, red capsicum and garlic for 3 – 4 minutes until soft. Stir in red wine, tomato purée and spices. Cook for 2 – 3 minutes. Stir in lentils and mix well. Season with salt and pepper.

3 In a mixing bowl, blend eggs, yoghurt and Parmesan cheese. Stir in nutmeg.

4 In a 35 cm x 22 cm oven dish, cover base with one-third of the eggplant and potato slices. Cover with half the lentil mixture. Make another layer of potato and eggplant, then cover with remainder of lentil mixture. Finish with remaining potato and eggplant slices.

4 Spread with topping and bake for about 30 minutes until top is lightly browned.

> **Winning tip**
> *This moussaka converts easily to a meat dish. Substitute about 400 g lean minced lamb or beef for the lentils. Brown the meat with the onion, then add the red capsicum, garlic, wine, purée, spices and seasonings. Provided you use sweet potatoes, this variation will fit the low-GI bill.*

chickpea and apple curry

serves 4

1 tablespoon virgin olive oil

1 tablespoon Madras curry powder

1 large onion, cut into quarters

2 tablespoons freshly grated ginger

4 cloves garlic

½ cup chopped coriander

1 x 425 g can chopped tomatoes

2 large green apples, peeled, cored and cut into thick slices

2 x 400 g can chickpeas, rinsed and drained

1 tablespoon fresh lemon juice

1 cup plain low-fat yoghurt

fresh coriander leaves for garnish

1 Heat oil in a saucepan and sauté curry powder over a medium heat for 1 minute. Add onion, ginger and garlic and cook for 2 – 3 minutes until onion starts to soften. Add coriander, tomatoes, apples and chickpeas.

2 Cover and cook for 20 – 25 minutes until apple is tender. Uncover and simmer for 5 minutes to reduce the sauce a little. Remove from heat and stir in lemon juice.

3 To serve, ladle the curry into bowls, top with a dollop of yoghurt and garnish with a few coriander leaves. Accompany with Basmati rice and steamed green vegetables and popadums.

GLYCAEMIC LOAD 1¼

Per serve	
Energy	1600 kJ
Protein	18 g
Fat	10 g
Carbohydrate	49 g
Fibre	14 g
GI	Low

fish tagine with chickpeas and potatoes

serves 4

Spice paste

1 tablespoon ground cumin

1 tablespoon ground coriander

2 tablespoons ground sweet paprika

2 cloves garlic

2 small red chillies, de-seeded

juice of 1 lemon

1 tablespoon virgin olive oil

150 g ripe tomatoes, de-seeded

Tagine

6 green onions, roughly chopped

200 g cooked chickpeas, drained

400 g waxy potatoes, cut into small cubes

1 cup crushed tomatoes

1 cup vegetable, chicken or fish stock

500 g firm white boneless fish fillets, cut into cubes

3 tablespoons plain low-fat yoghurt

½ cup coriander leaves for garnish

1 Place cumin, coriander, paprika, garlic, chilli, lemon juice, oil and tomatoes in a food processor and blend to a paste.

2 In a deep saucepan, add spice mix and cook for 2 – 3 minutes over a high heat. Stir in green onions, chickpeas, potatoes, tomatoes and stock. Cover and cook for 8 – 10 minutes, until potatoes are just tender.

3 Stir in cubed fish and cover. Cook for a further 5 – 8 minutes, until fish is cooked through. Ladle into bowls, garnish with coriander leaves and serve immediately with yoghurt on the side.

GLYCAEMIC LOAD 1

Per serve	
Energy	1450 kJ
Protein	44 g
Fat	9 g
Carbohydrate	26 g
Fibre	6 g
GI	Low

roast rack of lamb with gratin of cannellini beans

serves 4

2 tablespoons virgin olive oil
1 onion, finely chopped
1 garlic clove, finely chopped
1 teaspoon fresh rosemary, finely chopped
2 x 400 g cans cannellini beans, drained and liquid reserved
1 tablespoon white balsamic vinegar
1 tablespoon fresh multigrain breadcrumbs
1 tablespoon Parmesan cheese
4 baby racks of lamb, trimmed of fat (about 3 chops per rack)
freshly ground black pepper

1 Preheat oven to 200°C. Heat 2 teaspoons olive oil and cook onion and garlic over a medium heat until soft. Add rosemary and cannellini beans and heat through over a high heat.

2 Transfer to a food processor. Add ½ tablespoon olive oil, balsamic vinegar and 3 tablespoons of reserved liquid. Purée until smooth.

3 Transfer mixture to a lightly greased ceramic baking dish and sprinkle with breadcrumbs and Parmesan cheese. Bake for about 20 minutes, until golden brown on top.

4 To cook the lamb, season with pepper and brush with remainder of oil. Place on baking tray and roast for 15 – 20 minutes, until cooked. Remove from oven and rest for 10 minutes before serving. Serve the lamb (3 chops per person) and gratin accompanied with steamed green vegetables or salad.

GLYCAEMIC LOAD 1¾

Per serve	
Energy	2260 kJ
Protein	42 g
Fat	16 g
Carbohydrate	59 g
Fibre	8 g
GI	Low

spicy mexican beans
with avocado and yoghurt

serves 4

1 tablespoon virgin olive oil

3 red onions, peeled and cut into chunks

2 cloves garlic, finely chopped

2 red capsicums, de-seeded and roughly chopped

2 teaspoons ground coriander

1 teaspoon ground cumin

1 – 1½ teaspoons ground spicy paprika

1 x 425 g can chopped tomatoes

2 x 450 g cans red kidney beans, drained and rinsed

1½ cups vegetable stock

4 tablespoons plain low-fat yoghurt

1 small firm avocado

1 tablespoon lemon juice

1 tablespoon coriander leaves

1 Heat oil in a saucepan and cook onion over a low heat for 3 – 4 minutes. Stir in garlic and capsicum and cook for a further 8 minutes until lightly browned. Stir in coriander, cumin and paprika and cook for 1 minute.

2 Add tomatoes, kidney beans and vegetable stock. Bring to the boil, then reduce heat and simmer for 20 minutes. Adjust seasoning if necessary.

3 Peel and chop the avocado, add lemon juice and mix. To serve, spoon bean mixture into bowls, top with yoghurt and diced avocado, and garnish with coriander leaves.

Winning tip
This spicy Mexican dish works well served in warmed taco shells or rolled up in soft enchiladas.

GLYCAEMIC LOAD 1¼

Per serve	
Energy	1720 kJ
Protein	18 g
Fat	15 g
Carbohydrate	40 g
Fibre	16 g
GI	Low

madras pork wraps with yoghurt and mint

serves 4 – 8

1 tablespoon canola oil
250 g lean minced pork
1 tablespoon Madras curry paste
1 red onion, finely chopped
salt
freshly ground black pepper
1 x 400 g can chickpeas or lentils, drained
2 tablespoons plain low-fat yoghurt
½ cup fresh mint leaves
4 slices mountain bread (cornmeal or wholemeal)
chilli sauce or fruit chutney to serve

1 Heat oil in a frypan or wok over a medium heat, add pork and stir-fry for 2 – 3 minutes. Lower heat and add curry paste and onion. Stir-fry for a further 2 minutes, then season with salt and pepper to taste.

2 Add chickpeas and cook for 4 – 5 minutes until heated through. Remove from heat and stir in yoghurt and mint.

3 Cut mountain bread slices in half and spread one end with a little of the pork mixture. Roll up and serve while still warm, with a small dish of chilli sauce or fruit chutney on the side.

GLYCAEMIC LOAD 1

Per serve	
Energy	1420 kJ
Protein	24 g
Fat	10 g
Carbohydrate	29 g
Fibre	7 g
GI	Low

mexican chicken, beans and avocado with crispy corn tortilla

serves 4

1 tablespoon virgin olive oil
1 onion, finely chopped
1 bunch fresh coriander, leaves and stalks finely chopped
1 small red chilli, de-seeded and finely chopped
2 red capsicums, de-seeded and finely chopped
1 green capsicum, de-seeded and finely chopped
3 cloves garlic, crushed
2 chicken breast halves, about 500 g
4 cups chicken stock
1 x 300 g can kidney beans, drained
1 large ripe avocado, peeled, stone removed, and cut into small cubes
juice of 1 lime
salt
freshly ground black pepper
oil spray
2 corn tortillas

1 In a saucepan, heat oil and add onion, ¾ of the coriander, chilli, capsicum and garlic. Cook over a gentle heat for 4 – 5 minutes, until soft, stirring occasionally. Add chicken breasts and 1 cup chicken stock. Poach chicken for about 15 minutes until tender. Remove with tongs and, using a sharp knife, shred the meat.
2 Pour remainder of stock into the saucepan and slowly bring to the boil. Stir in beans and heat through. Add chicken and simmer for 2 – 4 minutes. Stir in avocado, lime juice and remaining coriander. Season to taste.
3 Heat a non-stick frypan and spray with oil. Cook corn tortillas, one at a time, over a high heat. Brown each side for 2 – 3 minutes. Remove from heat and cut into thin strips. Spoon chicken into bowls and serve with crispy fried tortillas strips.

GLYCAEMIC LOAD 1

Per serve	
Energy	2180 kJ
Protein	38 g
Fat	26 g
Carbohydrate	24 g
Fibre	9 g
GI	Low

creole beef, corn and borlotti bean bake

serves 4

2 tablespoons virgin olive oil

2 onlons, finely chopped

400 g lean minced beef

1 tomato, roughly chopped

¼ teaspoon ground cumin

¼ teaspoon ground cinnamon

100 g canned Borlotti beans, drained and rinsed

½ cup beef stock

6 black olives, stones removed and roughly chopped

2 tablespoons flat-leaf parsley, chopped

2 tablespoons raisins, roughly chopped

1 small green onion, finely chopped

1 x 400 g can corn kernels or corn from 4 fresh ears

2 omega-enriched eggs, beaten with 1 tablespoon plain flour

salt

freshly ground black pepper

1 Preheat oven to 180°C. Heat oil in a saucepan and cook onion over a low heat for about 4 minutes, until soft. Add beef, tomato, cumin and cinnamon and cook until meat has browned. Stir in Borlotti beans and stock and bring to the boil. Reduce heat and simmer, covered, for 10 minutes.

2 Remove from heat and stir in olives, parsley and raisins. Place in a greased baking dish of about 6-cup capacity.

3 In a food processor, blend green onion, corn kernels and egg and flour mixture. Season to taste and spread over cooked beef mixture. Bake for 45 – 50 minutes until topping is lightly browned. Serve immediately, accompanied with a green salad.

Winning tip
This unusual topping can be used with other meat or bean dishes. Add diced fresh green or red chilli for extra spice.

GLYCAEMIC LOAD 1

Per serve	
Energy	1820 kJ
Protein	31 g
Fat	18 g
Carbohydrate	38 g
Fibre	6 g
GI	Low

chilli con carne with mountain bread wraps

serves 4

1 tablespoon light olive oil

2 onions, finely chopped

500 g lean minced beef

1 teaspoon cumin seeds

1 teaspoon ground cinnamon

1 teaspoon chilli paste

1 x 425 g can tomatoes, roughly chopped

½ cup red wine

1 x 400 g can red kidney beans, drained and rinsed

3 tablespoons fresh parsley, finely chopped

1 tablespoon fresh basil, finely chopped

¼ cup stuffed green olives, finely chopped

4 wholemeal or barley mountain bread wraps

¼ cup cheddar cheese, grated

4 tomatoes, roughly chopped

1 In a large saucepan, heat oil and cook onion over a gentle heat until soft. Add beef and cook until browned.

2 Add cumin seeds, cinnamon and chilli paste and cook for 2 minutes. Stir in tomatoes and wine. Bring to the boil then simmer for 15 minutes to reduce the sauce a little. Add kidney beans, parsley, basil and olives and cook for another 5 minutes to heat through.

3 Spoon onto mountain bread, top with cheddar cheese and chopped tomatoes, then roll up and serve immediately. Alternatively, spoon filling into warmed taco shells and top with cheddar cheese.

GLYCAEMIC LOAD 1½

Per serve	
Energy	2080 kJ
Protein	41 g
Fat	19 g
Carbohydrate	37 g
Fibre	13 g
GI	Low

desserts

We love desserts and have had a superb time creating alternatives to the traditional Australian end-of-meal treat of canned fruit and ice cream. When you think about it, though, that course does have some nutritional pluses. Fruit and dairy are foods that many of us lack.

In considering a meal's total carbohydrates, or Glycaemic Load, it is important to appreciate the impact of dessert. There are times when we really want a dessert, whether it's because we have a sweet tooth or for social reasons. If this is the case, go for fewer carbohydrates in the main part of the meal to keep your carbs in balance.

And drop any guilt. We've created an array of wonderfully toothsome desserts, using nutritious ingredients with minimised fat levels. Enjoy!

contents

baked plums with walnut topping

serves 4

8 ripe plums
2 tablespoons apple concentrate
¼ cup water
⅓ cup soft brown wholegrain breadcrumbs
2 tablespoons soft brown sugar or 2 tablespoons Fruisana
⅓ cup walnuts, roughly chopped

1 Preheat oven to 200°C. Cut plums in half and remove stones. Place in a shallow baking dish, cut side up.
2 Combine apple concentrate and water and pour over plums. Mix breadcrumbs, sugar or Fruisana, and walnuts. Spoon over fruit.
3 Bake for 30 minutes or until tender. Remove from oven and serve immediately, accompanied with low-fat ice cream or low-fat honey yoghurt.

> *Winning tip*
> *Combinations of stone fruits, such as peaches, apricots or nectarines, are also delicious with this recipe.*

GLYCAEMIC LOAD ¾

WITH SUGAR

GLYCAEMIC LOAD ½

WITH FRUISANA

Per serve	
Energy	700 kJ
Protein	2 g
Fat	6 g
Carbohydrate	23 g
Fibre	3 g
GI	Low

baked pears with muscat and raisins

serves 4

4 ripe Bosc pears
2 tablespoons honey
½ cup raisins
1 cup Muscat or apple syrup or grape juice

1 Preheat oven to 180°C. Peel pears, cut in half and core. Warm honey and brush over pears.
2 Heat a non-stick frypan and lightly spray with oil. Cook pears, cut side down, for 3 – 4 minutes until browned. Remove to a ceramic baking dish.
3 Place raisins and Muscat in the frypan and bring to the boil. Pour over pears and bake for 20 minutes until pears are tender. Serve warm, accompanied with low-fat vanilla or honey yoghurt.

GLYCAEMIC LOAD 2½

Per serve	
Energy	1010 kJ
Protein	1 g
Fat	neg
Carbohydrate	58 g
Fibre	5 g
GI	Low

macerated berry and yoghurt parfait

serves 4

400 g fresh berries (strawberries, blueberries,
   raspberries, blackberries)
2 tablespoons balsamic vinegar
1 tablespoon brown sugar or 1 tablespoon Fruisana
4 amaretti biscuits
225 ml low-fat yoghurt, fruit or plain

1 Combine berries in a medium-sized bowl and sprinkle over balsamic vinegar and brown sugar or Fruisana. Stand, stirring occasionally, for about 30 minutes, until berries soften and start to release their juices.
2 Place amaretti biscuits in a plastic bag and smash with a rolling pin until roughly crushed. Layer berries with yoghurt in parfait glasses and top with a sprinkling of crushed amaretti biscuits. Refrigerate for 3 hours before serving.

GLYCAEMIC LOAD ½
WITH SUGAR

GLYCAEMIC LOAD ¼
WITH FRUISANA

Per serve	
Energy	400 kJ
Protein	4 g
Fat	2 g
Carbohydrate	13 g
Fibre	2 g
GI	Low

semolina soufflés with marinated strawberries

serves 4

1½ cups low-fat milk

⅓ cup (75 g) fine semolina

3 tablespoons caster sugar or 3 tablespoons Fruisana

½ teaspoon vanilla extract

zest of large orange or lemon

1 omega-enriched egg, separated

2 tablespoons Grand Marnier

1 cup finely chopped strawberries

icing sugar to decorate

1 tablespoon toasted almond flakes

1 Preheat oven to 180°C. Line 4 flat-bottomed 150 ml-capacity soufflé dishes with oven-bake paper.

2 Place milk, semolina and caster sugar or Fruisana in a saucepan and heat, stirring continuously, until mixture boils. Cook for a further minute until thickened. Add vanilla extract and zest. Remove from heat and let stand, covered with a sheet of plastic wrap or oven-bake paper to prevent a skin forming. Allow to cool.

3 When semolina mixture is cool, stir in egg yolk. Lightly whisk egg white until stiff and gently fold through. Spoon into soufflé dishes and stand in a larger baking dish. Fill with enough boiling water to come halfway up sides of soufflé dishes. Place in oven and cook for about 15 – 20 minutes.

4 Pour Grand Marnier over strawberries and leave to marinate until ready to serve. Remove soufflés from oven and run knife around sides of dishes to ease them out. Turn onto individual serving plates and remove oven-bake paper. To serve, spoon strawberries around soufflés, top with toasted almond flakes and dust with icing sugar.

GLYCAEMIC LOAD 1¼   GLYCAEMIC LOAD ¾

WITH SUGAR   WITH FRUISANA

Per serve	
Energy	850 kJ
Protein	9 g
Fat	3 g
Carbohydrate	31 g
Fibre	1 g
GI with sugar	Med
GI with Fruisana	Low

marinated orange segments with chocolate and orange mousse

serves 4

4 oranges, pith and skin removed, thinly sliced
1 tablespoon mint, finely chopped
2 – 3 tablespoons Grand Marnier
2 tablespoons orange juice
300 g silken tofu, drained
¼ cup quality cocoa powder
1 tablespoon maple syrup
½ tablespoon molasses
grated zest of 1 large orange
1 teaspoon vanilla extract
fresh mint leaves

1 Place orange slices in a bowl. Add mint and Grand Marnier and stir well. Refrigerate for 30 minutes.
2 In a food processor blend orange juice, silken tofu, cocoa, maple syrup, molasses, orange zest and vanilla extract until smooth and creamy. Refrigerate until ready to serve.
3 To serve, arrange a circle of orange slices on each of 4 individual plates and place a dessertspoon of chocolate mousse in the middle of each one. Decorate with a sprig of fresh mint leaves.

> **Winning tip**
> *Make coffee mousse by omitting the marinated oranges and blending the silken tofu with 1 tablespoon maple syrup, 2 tablespoons strong black coffee and 1 tablespoon Crème de Cacao or Kahlua. Serve with berries.*

GLYCAEMIC LOAD ½

Per serve	
Energy	930 kJ
Protein	11 g
Fat	6 g
Carbohydrate	25 g
Fibre	4 g
GI	Low

cardamom-scented custard pots

serves 8

500 g reduced-fat ricotta or cottage cheese
½ cup low-fat condensed milk
4 tablespoons plain low-fat yoghurt
½ teaspoon ground cardamom
2 tablespoons almond flakes

1 Preheat oven to 175°C. Combine ricotta cheese, condensed milk and yoghurt in a food processor. Stir in cardamom. Spoon mixture into 8 lightly oiled 125 ml ramekin dishes. Sprinkle tops with almond flakes.
2 Stand ramekins in a large baking dish and fill with enough hot water to reach about ¾ of the way up the sides. Bake for 20 minutes until set, then cool. Serve cold with slices of fresh or poached seasonal fruit.

GLYCAEMIC LOAD 1½

Per serve	
Energy	680 kJ
Protein	9 g
Fat	7 g
Carbohydrate	14 g
Fibre	Negligible
GI	Low

yoghurt and coconut custards with poached apricots

serves 4

125 g dried apricots, roughly chopped

1 tablespoon sugar or 1 tablespoon Fruisana

1 cup water

400 ml low-fat coconut milk

2 tablespoons caster sugar or 2 tablespoons Fruisana

30 g rice flour

200 g plain low-fat yoghurt

1 tablespoon shredded coconut, lightly toasted, for garnish

1 Place dried apricots in a saucepan with sugar or Fruisana and water. Bring to the boil and cook for about 20 minutes over a low heat, until tender, and the water has reduced to a syrup. Remove from heat and cool.

2 Heat coconut milk in a saucepan and whisk in caster sugar or Fruisana and rice flour. Slowly bring to the boil, gently whisking, until mixture thickens. Remove from the heat and cool.

3 Transfer coconut milk mixture to a food processor. Add yoghurt and half the apricots and blend. Spoon into 4 serving bowls and chill for 1 hour. To serve, top with remaining apricots and garnish with shredded coconut.

> **Winning tip**
> Using your blood glucose monitor, check the reduction in blood glucose levels when using Fruisana instead of sugar.

GLYCAEMIC LOAD 1¼
WITH SUGAR

GLYCAEMIC LOAD ¾
WITH FRUISANA

Per serve	
Energy	1100 kJ
Protein	6 g
Fat	6 g
Carbohydrate	45 g
Fibre	4 g
GI	Low

crêpe roll-ups with glacé fruit and chocolate filling

serves 4 (makes about 8 crêpes)

1 whole omega-enriched egg plus 1 omega-enriched egg yolk
300 ml low-fat milk
100 g plain flour
pinch of salt
1 tablespoon light olive oil plus extra for frying

Filling
300 g low-fat ricotta cheese
2 tablespoons plain low-fat yoghurt
4 tablespoons finely chopped glacé peach, pear or pineapple
1 tablespoon cocoa powder
2 tablespoons orange liqueur (Grand Marnier, Cointreau or orange juice)
icing sugar for decoration

1 Whisk egg plus egg yolk with half the milk. Gradually beat in sifted flour until combined. Slowly beat in remainder of milk then beat in oil. Batter should be quite thin and free of lumps. Rest for 30 minutes.
2 In a large bowl, fold together all filling ingredients until combined. Refrigerate.
3 Heat a non-stick frypan or crêpe pan and cook thin pancakes. Spread each pancake with filling.
Roll up tightly and cut each roll-up into pieces of 3 or 4 finger widths.
4 Arrange on a lightly greased ceramic oven-to-table baking dish and crisp in a very hot oven for a few minutes – alternatively, leave at room temperature. Serve with a dusting of icing sugar.

GLYCAEMIC LOAD 1

Per serve	
Energy	1290 kJ
Protein	17 g
Fat	10 g
Carbohydrate	32 g
Fibre	1 g
GI	Low

cherry cheese strudel

serves 6

400 g low-fat ricotta cheese

1 omega-enriched egg plus 1 omega-enriched egg yolk, lightly beaten

½ cup dry wholegrain breadcrumbs

3 tablespoons caster sugar or 3 tablespoons Fruisana

¾ cup pitted canned cherries, well drained

6 sheets of filo pastry

oil for spraying filo sheets

¼ cup chopped roasted walnuts

icing sugar for dusting

1 Preheat oven to 200°C. In a mixing bowl, fold together ricotta cheese, egg, breadcrumbs and caster sugar or Fruisana. Stir in cherries. Refrigerate until ready to use.

2 On a sheet of oven-bake paper, spread a sheet of filo pastry, short side towards you. Spray with a little oil and sprinkle with a few walnuts. Cover with second sheet of filo pastry, spray with oil and sprinkle with more walnuts. Continue until all filo sheets have been used.

3 Spoon ricotta mixture in a thick log along short side of prepared filo sheets, keeping the edges clear. Fold long sides of filo over filling. Carefully roll up to form a log-shaped packet. Slide onto a baking tray and dust with icing sugar.

4 Bake in oven for 15 minutes. Reduce oven temperature to 180°C and cook for a further 15 – 20 minutes until pastry is brown and crisp. Remove from oven and cool a little before cutting with a serrated knife. To serve, dust with icing sugar and accompany with low-fat ice cream.

GLYCAEMIC LOAD ¾   **GLYCAEMIC LOAD ½**

WITH SUGAR   WITH FRUISANA

Per serve	
Energy	900 kJ
Protein	10 g
Fat	10 g
Carbohydrate	21 g
Fibre	1 g
GI	Low

pear and almond tart

serves 6

130 g self-raising flour

35 g ground almonds

⅓ cup caster sugar or ⅓ cup Fruisana

4 tablespoons light olive oil

1 cup buttermilk

2 omega-enriched eggs

1 teaspoon vanilla extract

2 ripe pears, peeled and cored

⅓ cup flaked almonds

icing sugar to dust

1 Preheat oven to 180°C. Line a 20 cm round fluted flan tin with oven-bake paper.

2 In a bowl, combine flour, ground almonds and sugar or Fruisana. In a separate bowl whisk oil, buttermilk, eggs and vanilla extract. Fold wet ingredients into dry ingredients.

3 Roughly chop one pear and stir through mixture, then pour into the flan tin.

4 Thinly slice the other pear and arrange over the top. Sprinkle with flaked almonds and lightly dust with icing sugar. Bake for 30 – 35 minutes until lightly browned and cooked through.

5 Cool a little in the tin before turning out. Dust with icing sugar and cut into wedges. Serve warm, accompanied with low-fat custard or honey yoghurt.

GLYCAEMIC LOAD 2   GLYCAEMIC LOAD 1½

WITH SUGAR   WITH FRUISANA

Per serve	
Energy	1750 kJ
Protein	10 g
Fat	23 g
Carbohydrate	44 g
Fibre	4 g
GI with sugar	Medium
GI with Fruisana	Low

little rhubarb
and strawberry cakes

makes 12 cakes

2 cups unbleached self-raising flour

1/3 cup brown sugar or 1/3 cup Fruisana

250 g strawberries, hulled and roughly chopped

200 g rhubarb, trimmed and roughly chopped

1 teaspoon vanilla extract

2 omega-enriched eggs

1 cup plain low-fat yoghurt

1/3 cup vegetable oil or light olive oil

2 tablespoons strawberry or blackcurrant jam
(warmed in the microwave or saucepan)

1 Preheat oven to 180°C. Lightly grease a 12-cup muffin tin.

2 In a bowl, mix flour, brown sugar or Fruisana, strawberries and rhubarb. In a separate bowl lightly whisk vanilla extract, eggs, yoghurt and oil. Pour wet ingredients into flour mixture and stir lightly until just combined.

3 Spoon batter into the prepared muffin tin. Bake for 20 minutes, then remove from oven. Brush with a little jam to glaze tops. Return to oven for a further 5 minutes. Remove from oven, rest for 5 minutes, then carefully turn out cakes onto a wire rack to cool. Serve warm or at room temperature, accompanied with low-fat ice cream.

GLYCAEMIC LOAD 1¼   GLYCAEMIC LOAD 1

WITH SUGAR   WITH FRUISANA

Per serve	
Energy	820 kJ
Protein	6 g
Fat	7 g
Carbohydrate	27 g
Fibre	2 g
GI with sugar	Medium
GI with Fruisana	Low

classic rice pudding

serves 8

4 cups low-fat milk
½ cup Doongara rice
2 large omega-enriched egg yolks
¼ cup brown sugar or ¼ cup Fruisana
1½ teaspoons vanilla extract

1 Place milk and rice in a large saucepan. Bring to the boil over a high heat, stirring continuously. Reduce heat to low and cover. Simmer for 15 minutes, stirring occasionally. Remove the lid and continue cooking, stirring occasionally until liquid has reduced by about ¼ and rice is tender.
2 Whisk egg yolks, sugar or Fruisana and vanilla extract. Slowly stir rice into egg mixture, then return to the saucepan. Cook over a low heat, stirring continuously, for about 5 minutes until thick and creamy.
3 Remove from heat, spoon into a bowl and cover with plastic wrap to prevent a skin forming. Cool to room temperature before serving.

Winning tip
Very recent research suggests that we need a good calcium intake so our bodies can effectively use up fat stores. So the more dairy-based dishes you enjoy, the easier it may be to control body fat.

GLYCAEMIC LOAD 1
WITH SUGAR

GLYCAEMIC LOAD ¾
WITH FRUISANA

Per serve	
Energy	600 kJ
Protein	8 g
Fat	1 g
Carbohydrate	25 g
Fibre	Negligible
GI	Low

raspberry parfait
rice pudding

serves 6

1 quantity of rice pudding (see facing page)
400 g fresh raspberries or blueberries
icing sugar for dusting

1 In 6 glass tumblers or bowls, layer rice pudding with
raspberries, finishing with a few raspberries on the top.
2 Dust with icing sugar to serve.

> **Winning tip**
> *This parfait can be made with poached rhubarb, plums,
> peaches or other seasonal fruit.*

GLYCAEMIC LOAD 1¼

WITH SUGAR

GLYCAEMIC LOAD 1

WITH FRUISANA

Per serve	
Energy	700 kJ
Protein	9 g
Fat	1 g
Carbohydrate	27 g
Fibre	2 g
GI	Low

ricotta fruit pudding with melba sauce

serves 8

8 shredded wheatmeal biscuits, crushed into crumbs
125 g reduced-fat cream cheese
500 g low-fat ricotta cheese
½ teaspoon vanilla extract
2 large omega-enriched eggs, lightly beaten
2 tablespoons apple juice concentrate
1 'snak pac' apple and blackcurrant purée or other berry purée
   (about 140 g)

Sauce
300 g fresh, canned or frozen raspberries (defrosted)

1 Preheat oven to 175°C. Lightly grease oven-to-table ceramic dish, about 20 cm round, and sprinkle with ⅔ of the biscuits.
2 Beat cream cheese, ricotta cheese, vanilla extract, eggs and apple juice concentrate until smooth. Swirl through fruit purée then spoon evenly into dish. Sprinkle with remaining biscuits.
3 Bake for 20 – 30 minutes until set. Remove from oven and cool. Blend raspberries with juice to a purée and sieve to remove seeds. To serve, spoon warm ricotta fruit pudding onto plates and pour over a little raspberry sauce.

GLYCAEMIC LOAD ¼

Per serve	
Energy	760 kJ
Protein	10 g
Fat	11 g
Carbohydrate	11 g
Fibre	<1 g
GI	Low

rhubarb bread pudding

serves 6

2 bunches rhubarb, trimmed and roughly chopped
   (approximately 600 g)
½ cup orange juice
2 tablespoons sugar or 2 tablespoons Fruisana
1 cup low-fat milk
3 omega-enriched eggs
1 teaspoon vanilla extract
1 tablespoon sugar or 1 tablespoon Fruisana
150 g stale Italian bread, cut into cubes (about 1 cup)
ground cinnamon for dusting
ground nutmeg for dusting

1 Preheat oven to 160°C. In a saucepan, mix rhubarb, orange juice and sugar or Fruisana. Cover and bring to the boil. Reduce heat and cook for about 5 minutes until rhubarb is soft.

2 Mix milk, eggs, vanilla extract and sugar or Fruisana. Place rhubarb in a baking dish, top with bread and pour over egg mixture. Dust with cinnamon and nutmeg. Cover and bake for 30 minutes. Uncover and bake for another 30 minutes to brown the top.

GLYCAEMIC LOAD 1   **GLYCAEMIC LOAD ¾**

WITH SUGAR   WITH FRUISANA

Per serve	
Energy	910 kJ
Protein	9 g
Fat	5 g
Carbohydrate	31 g
Fibre	4 g
GI with sugar	Medium
GI with Fruisana	Low

prune and walnut bread

makes 16 – 20 thin slices

275 ml buttermilk
2 tablespoons treacle
1¼ cups self-raising flour
1¼ cups wholemeal flour
½ teaspoon bicarbonate of soda
½ cup walnuts, chopped
½ cup stoned prunes, chopped

1 Preheat oven to 200°C. Lightly grease a 25 cm x 15 cm loaf tin and line with oven-bake paper. Warm buttermilk and treacle in a saucepan and stir until treacle has melted. Cool a little.

2 In a bowl, combine self-raising flour, wholemeal flour, bicarbonate of soda, walnuts and prunes. Stir in buttermilk mixture to form a soft dough.

3 Spoon into prepared loaf tin and bake for 30 – 35 minutes until firm and cooked through. Cool in the tin then turn out onto a rack. Serve with low-fat ricotta cheese or thin slices of Parmesan cheese, cheddar or soft blue-vein cheese.

GLYCAEMIC LOAD ¾

Per serve	
Energy	400 kJ
Protein	3 g
Fat	2 g
Carbohydrate	15 g
Fibre	1 g
GI	Medium

hazelnut and lemon cake

serves 6

3 large omega-enriched eggs, separated
50 g soft brown sugar or 50 g Fruisana
3 tablespoons plain low-fat yoghurt
100 g hazelnuts, roasted and ground into coarse crumbs.
60 g roasted dry wholemeal breadcrumbs
shredded zest of 1 lemon
icing sugar for dusting

1 Preheat oven to 180°C. Line the base of a 20 cm spring-form cake tin with oven-bake paper.
2 In a mixing bowl, whisk egg yolks and sugar or Fruisana with an electric beater for 3–4 minutes until light and creamy. Carefully stir in yoghurt, nuts, breadcrumbs and lemon zest.
3 In another bowl, whisk egg whites until stiff. Fold into cake batter and pour into prepared tin. Bake for 30 – 35 minutes, until a skewer inserted in the centre comes out clean.
4 Remove cake onto a wire rack and cool. To serve, dust with icing sugar and accompany with honey-flavoured yoghurt and canned or fresh fruit.

GLYCAEMIC LOAD ½   GLYCAEMIC LOAD ¼

WITH SUGAR   WITH FRUISANA

Per serve	
Energy	930 kJ
Protein	7 g
Fat	15 g
Carbohydrate	14 g
Fibre	2 g
GI	Low

semolina cake with poached apples or pears

serves 8

2 omega-enriched eggs

125 g castor sugar or 125 g Fruisana

1 teaspoon vanilla extract

½ cup vegetable oil

80 ml orange juice plus 1 extra cup for poaching

zest of 1 small orange

150 g fine semolina

80 g plain flour

2 teaspoons baking powder

4 apples or 4 pears, peeled, cored and cut into 8 segments

1 teaspoon ginger grated

1 Preheat oven to 180°C and line the base of a 22 cm spring-form tin with oven-bake paper. Using an electric mixer beat the eggs, vanilla extract and castor sugar or Fruisana until pale and slightly thickened (3 – 4 minutes). Beat in the oil, 80 ml orange juice and orange zest.

2 In bowl sift together semolina, flour and baking powder, then fold into the egg mixture. Pour into tin. Bake for 30 – 35 minutes or until a skewer comes out clean when inserted. Rest for 5 minutes then turn out onto wire cooling rack.

3 While the cake is cooling, place the apple or pear slices into saucepan with 1 cup orange juice and the grated ginger. Poach gently for about 10 minutes, until the fruit is just cooked. Transfer to a bowl, add remaining liquid and refrigerate.

4 Serve slices of cake with fruit. Drizzle over remaining poaching liquid and accompany with low-fat ice cream for taste and to add carbohydrate.

GLYCAEMIC LOAD 1

WITH SUGAR

GLYCAEMIC LOAD ¾

WITH FRUISANA

Per serve	
Energy	870 kJ
Protein	5 g
Fat	7 g
Carbohydrate	30 g
Fibre	2 g
GI	Low

the GI story

For some years, diabetics were encouraged to believe that consuming the same quantity (number of grams) of carbohydrate in one food would have the same effect on their blood glucose levels (BGLs) as an equal amount of carbohydrate in any other food. However, when better blood glucose testing equipment became available, it revealed that there could be enormous variations in the rate at which glucose is released into the blood, even if the quantities of different carbohydrates were the same.

Further investigations have revealed that a number of factors can cause these variations to occur:

- type of starch/sugar in food
- degree of gelatinisation (stickiness) of starch
- physical form of food
- particle shape of food
- method of cooking
- presence of certain fibres
- acidity or acid added
- fat content or fat added.

To measure the variation in impact of different carbohydrates on BGLs, a benchmark was necessary. This was set by measuring the rate of glucose release in the body after consuming pure glucose. The result was given a nominal rating of 100. Then the rate of glucose release from consuming various carbohydrates was measured and compared with that benchmark. This gave each carbohydrate a rating known as the Glycaemic Index (GI), from which a hierarchy of carbohydrates could be created (see GI food listing, on page 155).

Using the GI system, a score of:

less than 55   indicates a low-GI food
between 55-70   indicates a medium-GI food
over 70   indicates a high-GI food.

Foods with *slower* rates of glucose release (or a low-GI) require less insulin to process the glucose, because the glucose is absorbed more slowly. Being less likely to overwhelm the metabolism, low-GI foods are less dependent on effective insulin for processing. Therefore eating the same quantity (number of grams) of carbohydrate food, but selecting a low-GI variety, will automatically reduce BGLs, since, with less glucose being released at one time, it is easier for whatever active insulin is present to process it. This explains why the old method of exchanging similar quantities of carbohydrate in one food with another could produce a radically different blood glucose effect, and thus didn't always work.

The variation in blood glucose impact between different carbohydrate foods is also beneficial because, if a food releases its glucose more slowly into the system, the food should be more sustaining than a similar amount of food with a higher GI. What a help when trying to eat less.

No wonder the world of low-GI foods took off. Unfortunately, this does not mean that, if a food has a low-GI, it is all right to eat as much as you like. Although a food may have a low-GI, it will still produce too much glucose for your body if eaten to excess!

To understand the impact of eating low-GI foods better, here is an example. A sandwich of two slices of bread contains approximately 30 g of carbohydrate. Using wholemeal bread, the sandwich would have a GI of about 70 (or a medium-GI), whereas, using wholegrain bread, the same sandwich would have a GI of about 45 (or a low-GI). If managing diabetes by diet alone, the simple substitution of wholegrain bread for wholemeal would effectively reduce your BGL and keep you feeling full for longer, making it easier to eat less.

Research also shows that reduced blood glucose fluctuations, resulting from eating lower-GI foods, are beneficial for everybody. Consuming lower-GI foods has been linked to reductions in the incidence of other diseases, such as heart disease and hypertension, hence the low-GI recipes in *Food for Every Body* are ideal for us all.

Where changing the type of bread in the sandwich becomes slightly more complicated is when diabetic medication or insulin is being used. As the dosage of insulin should have been programmed to 'cope' with an expected level of glucose within the system, eating similar quantities but with a different GI level and Glycaemic Load may reduce your glucose level too much, unless the dosage is modified. *So, if you are on medication, check with your health practitioner first, before altering your diet significantly.*

A method of quantifying the impact on blood glucose was needed. Hence the development of the concept of Glycaemic Load for carbohydrates. This was calculated by multiplying the GI of a food by the quantity (number of grams) of carbohydrate in it. The product was then divided by 100.

If we take the example of the sandwich again, using this system, a wholemeal sandwich would have a Glycaemic Load of 30 (g) x 70 (GI)/100 or 21, whereas a wholegrain sandwich would have a Glycaemic Load of 30 (g) x 45 (GI)/100 or 13.5.

In other words, the wholegrain sandwich delivers almost 50 per cent less Glycaemic Load than the wholemeal sandwich. It should be noted, however, that this does not mean that to keep the same blood glucose effect you can simply switch to wholegrain bread and then eat 50 per cent more (3 slices). Three slices of wholegrain would still contain the kilojoules of three slices of any type of bread, rather than two, so it would be counterproductive by producing extra tummy fat.

While low-GI foods are better for BGLs than medium- or high-GI foods, the quantity consumed is still vitally important. The best way to check whether your glucose intake is appropriate is to use your blood glucose monitor regularly.

Generic list of low-GI foods

Breads	*wholegrain ('crack-your-teeth') varieties; all breads of the Bürgen™ style; dark pumpernickel; pita breads (brown and white); all fruit loaf breads*
Biscuits	*9-grain Vita-Weat™; Shredded Wheatmeal™; Snac Right™*
Cereals	*rolled oats; untoasted muesli; oat-based cereals; All Bran™ (and variants); Mini Wheats™; Special K™; Vita Brits™*
Rice	*Basmati; 'Clever' fast-cooking rice, using the Doongara™ rice*
Pasta	*all types and shapes*
Other grains	*burghul and other cracked wheats; barley*
Legumes	*baked beans; kidney beans; cannellini beans; chickpeas; soybeans; lentils (all types)*
Potatoes	*sweet potato; new potatoes (only grown in Tasmania; elsewhere in Australia, these are only available in cans)*
Fruits	*all fruits are good carbohydrates, but the further south a fruit is naturally grown, the slower it will release its glucose to the system. Slow fruits start with the southern bananas.*
Dairy	*all dairy foods are low-GI, so low-fat varieties have three winning aspects – high calcium levels, good slow energy and reduced fats.*

GI foods list
Examples of specific GI ratings *These foods are high in fat

Low-GI (less than 55)		Medium-GI (55–70)		High-GI (70+)	
Peanuts*	14	Banana	55	Corn chips*	72
Soybeans	19	Mango	55	Watermelon	72
Fructose	23	Sweet corn	55	Bagel	72
Milk	25	Oatmeal biscuit	55	Sultana Bran™	73
Yoghurt fruit	33	Jatz cracker™*	55	Pumpkin	75
Cooked lentils,					
kidney beans etc	30-38	Muesli, untoasted	56	French fries	75
Pastas/noodles	32-46	Pita bread	57	Rice, brown	76
Dried apricot	32	Basmati rice	58	Waffles	76
Apple	38	Ice cream (average)*	61	Coco Pops™	77
Pear	39	New potatoes	62	Gatorade™	78
Plum	39	Beetroot	64	Water crackers	78
Peach	42	Rockmelon	65	Jelly beans	78
Orange	44	Sucrose (sugar)	65	Puffed crispbreads	81
Muesli/oats	42-44	Pineapple	66	Rice bubbles	83
Grapes	46	Croissant*	67	Pretzels	83
Fruit loaf	47	Wholemeal bread	69	Potatoes	85
Baked beans	48	Taco shell	68	Rice, short grain	87
Peas	48	Weetbix	69	Parsnip	97
Buckwheat	54	Sao crackers™	70	Glucose	100
Sweet potato	54	White bread	70	Maltose	105

These figures are reproduced from The Glucose Revolution, Assoc. Prof. J. Brand-Miller, K. Foster-Powell, and S. Colagiuri (Hodder Headline Australia, 1996) with the permission of the authors.
Go to www.glycemicindex.com for the latest testing results.

more about fat

We are advocating the benefits of moderating the fats eaten as part of any healthy eating programme. Fats are quite a complex topic. To begin with, they are vital for life. Apart from being the most concentrated energy source that exists, various fats:

- are incorporated into virtually every cell in the body
- are the starter materials for a number of key hormones
- act as insulation and protection to the body's organs and structures
- are essential to enable nutrients such as fat-soluble vitamins and antioxidants to move through the body.

And last, but not least, fats add to the taste of food!

Fat Qualities

Different food fats are made up of various combinations and sizes of the base unit called fatty acids. These are joined into different configurations, the size and shape of which determine how they function in the body.

> *Saturated fatty acid:*
> *fatty acid chain is completely straight*
> *Monounsaturated fatty acid chain:*
> *has one twist in the chain fatty acid:*
> *Polyunsaturated fatty acid:*
> *fatty acid chain has more than one twist in the chain*

Fat actions

Put simply, the different shapes of the various fatty acids determine their effects on the body. Food fats are described by the predominant fatty acid. Remember that you need some fat everyday, both fats found naturally in foods and those added in cooking.

Saturated fats (straight)

These are the hardest for the human body to process and are most likely to be stored as 'tummy' fat. They are said to stimulate the 'clogging' low-density lipoprotein (LDL) cholesterol, make arteries rigid, predispose to Type II diabetes and promote obesity. They are found in animal fats, such as butter, cream and meat fats, as well as in oils such as coconut and peanut.

Monounsaturated fats (one twist)

These are considered to be more neutral in effect than saturated fats. If monounsaturated fats are used to replace saturated fats, they appear to:

- reduce the production of the harmful LDL cholesterol
- increase the helpful high-density lipoprotein (HDL) cholesterol
- improve blood glucose control when the mono-unsaturated proportion of the total fat intake of a food is over 40 per cent (as in most *Food for Every Body* recipes).

The well-known monounsaturated foods are olives (olive oil) and canola oil, which is why we use these oils.

Polyunsaturated fats (more than one twist)

These are grouped according to where the first twist occurs. By far the two largest groups are those known as the omega-3 polyunsaturated fats (first 'twist' occurs three units from the tail end) and omega-6 polyunsaturated fats (first 'twist' occurs six units from the tail).

These omega fats can be further classified according to their chain length. The longer chain ones, those with more than 18 units, have quite differing effects on the body.

Humans cannot manufacture the extremely important omega-3 or 6 fat shapes from stored fat, so it is essential these fats are eaten daily – hence their name 'essential fats'.

Shape and chain length trigger differing effects, the major dietary ones being:

- omega-3 long chain (20 and 22 units) known respectively as Eicosapentaenoic acid (EPA) and Docosahexaenoic acid (DHA). Both are found only in animal foods and are essential as building bricks for all cell membranes. Their anti-inflammatory properties work throughout our bodies, affecting everything from joints to blood vessels, ageing to new cell division. They may also be protective against some of the long-term stressors of diabetes.

The best omega food sources in descending order of content	
For long omega-3s (EPAs)	*Deep sea fish (e.g. sardines, mackerel, salmon, swordfish, mullet, John Dory, snapper and trevally); seafood (e.g. mussels, oysters); Omega-3 enriched foods; lean game, pork, beef and lamb*
For shorter omega-3s (DHAs)	*Linseed oil, canola oil, olive oil, walnut oil, soybean oil; soybeans and wheatgerm; legumes; dark green leafy vegetables*
For omega-6s	*Sunflower oil, safflower oil, corn oil, sesame oil, grapeseed oil, 'vegetable oils'; sunflower and sesame seeds; breads; cereals*

As oily fish is the best food source, it is recommended that we all eat at least two fish meals per week.

- omega-3 short chain (18 or less units) – found in seeds, pulses and dark green vegetables – can be converted by the body into the more active long-chain fatty acids. Unfortunately, the process is not terribly efficient, so you need to include some of the EPAs and DHAs in your foods to get adequate amounts.
- omega-6 long chain and short chain reduce levels of the harmful LDL cholesterol but, unfortunately, if they are the only fat in the diet, they can reduce the good HDL cholesterol even more. So although including some in the diet is beneficial, too much may be harmful if no other fat sources are also eaten.

Cholesterol

This is a complex fatty substance made by animals, not plants. Humans manufacture over 1000 milligrams per day, mainly in the liver, from where it is used in:

- cell membranes
- hormones
- digestive juices
- nerve coating.

We have gradually come to understand what the major triggers are for cholesterol production in humans. These are not, as previously thought, cholesterol from certain foods, but that pesky 'tummy fat' and excessive consumption of saturated food fats. So, if you follow the approach we take in *Food for Every Body*, eggs, liver and kidneys are back on the menu – in moderation.

Our liver produces five types of blood cholesterol, but the major ones are:

- HDL, which can remove cholesterol from blood
- LDL, which is more likely to be deposited on artery walls, leading to the blockages in heart disease.

Basically, the more HDL cholesterol you have, the better. To increase HDL production, the best advice is:

- keep moving
- control excessive fat intake
- use more of the preferred oil sources.

Triglycerides

These fats are always present in blood because the body manufactures them regularly. High levels of triglycerides may suppress HDL manufacture and are another risk associated with increased heart disease. Over-eating or being overweight will stimulate production of triglycerides.

index